GRADE
7

The 2005 & 2006 Syllabus requirements, especially th sight-reading. Attention sh Notices on the inside front c any changes.

The syllabus is obtainable from music retailers or from the Services Department, The Associated Board of the Royal Schools of Music, 24 Portland Place, London W1B 1LU, United Kingdom (please send a stamped addressed C5 (162mm x 229mm) envelope).

In exam centres outside the UK, information and syllabuses may be obtained from the Local Representative.

CONTENTS

Where appropriate, pieces in this volume have been checked with original source material and edited as necessary for instructional purposes. Any editorial additions to the texts are given in small print, within square brackets, or – in the case of slurs and ties – in the form ⌢. Fingering, phrasing, pedalling, metronome marks and the editorial realization of ornaments (where given) are for guidance only; they are not comprehensive or obligatory.

Editor for the Associated Board: **Richard Jones**

DO NOT PHOTOCOPY © MUSIC

Alternative pieces for this grade

Music origination by Barnes Music Engraving Ltd.
Cover by Økvik Design.
Printed in Great Britain by Headley Brothers Ltd, The Invicta Press, Ashford, Kent.

Allegro

Second movement from Suite No. 2 in F, HWV 427

HANDEL

The Suite in F, HWV 427, from which this Allegro is drawn, is the second of the eight celebrated suites that Handel published in 1720. For these suites he made his own choice of the best of the keyboard music that he had composed in earlier years. Despite its name, the second suite is not really a dance suite at all but rather a keyboard version of the instrumental form *sonata da chiesa*. Accordingly, the Allegro is written in the fluent, violinistic Italian style of the time rather than in the more florid French style that tends to prevail in keyboard suites. Dynamics are left to the player's discretion. Quavers might be lightly detached.

Sources: autograph MS, British Library, R.M.20.g.14.; *Suites de pièces pour le clavecin* (London, 1720)

Adapted from Handel: *Eight Great Suites*, Book I, edited by Richard Jones (Associated Board)

For Johnny Mehegan
June 6, 1920
No. 2 from *Four Anniversaries*

BERNSTEIN

The American composer, conductor and pianist Leonard Bernstein (1918–90) wrote three sets of short piano pieces to celebrate the birthdays of friends and acquaintances. The piece dedicated to Johnny Mehegan, the jazz educator, writer and pianist, is drawn from the second set, which was published in 1948.

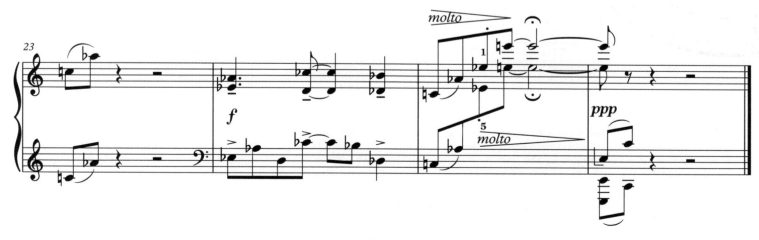

Contents

Quick Reference Things to Do

Would you like inspiration on family things to do and days out? This guide is filled with ideas; from cinemas to museums; sculpture parks to forest walks. Whether you live in Brighton or are just visiting, you will find a wealth of information in these pages.

There is always Brighton seafront, with its candy floss and pebble beach or wander over the beautiful South Downs. You can visit castles, pretty villages, indoor soft play centres or galleries. Or go swimming, take a tractor ride at a farm or a fun fair ride on the Palace Pier.

Feel the breeze taking an under cliff walk; let you child dip their toes in a seafront paddling pool or see the Llamas and animals in wildlife parks. Being a parent is busy enough so I hope that this guide may make life a bit easier!

Top 10 Family Favourites

1. **Discover nature & history:** Use real old pennies in the Vintage Penny Palace, see the strange masks and puppets at the Brighton Museum & Art Gallery or the Wizards Attic of toys at the Hove Museum (p19); wonder at the jellyfish and sharks at the Sealife Centre (p6).
2. **Summer swims:** Splash about in an outdoor pool in the summer, like The Pells in Lewes, Kings Road in Brighton (p67).
3. **The South Downs:** Climb the rolling chalk hills at Chanctonbury or Cissbury Ring; the cliffs at Birling Gap; or follow the river Adur (p47).
4. **Marvel at the Llamas or Meerkats:** Alpaca Llamas at the Llama Park or see the Red pandas, penguins and monkeys at Drusillas Park is (p61).
5. **Seasonal fun:** Visit the Lambs in Spring at Seven Sisters Sheep Centre (p61); run through the blue haze of bluebell woods, or kick up gold autumn leaves in (p39). For summer fun try the Brighton Festival or Children's Parade (p77). In winter there is ice skating at the Royal Pavilion.
6. **Saturday Movies:** Many cinemas have a low cost Kids Saturday club (p17).
7. **Take a train or bus for an adventure:** Train to Stanmer or Lewes (p53); Breeze bus to Devil's Dyke (p52) or a steam train in the Nene Valley (p36).
8. **Take the Volks Railway and explore the rockpools:** the great little railway takes you to Blackrock pools and beaches by Brighton Marina (p10).
9. **Find objects** left behind on a trail with geocache or go on a treasure hunt (p46).
10. **Run around and picnic in the Woods; in** Stanmer Park, Brighton or Kingley Vale near Chichester (p59).

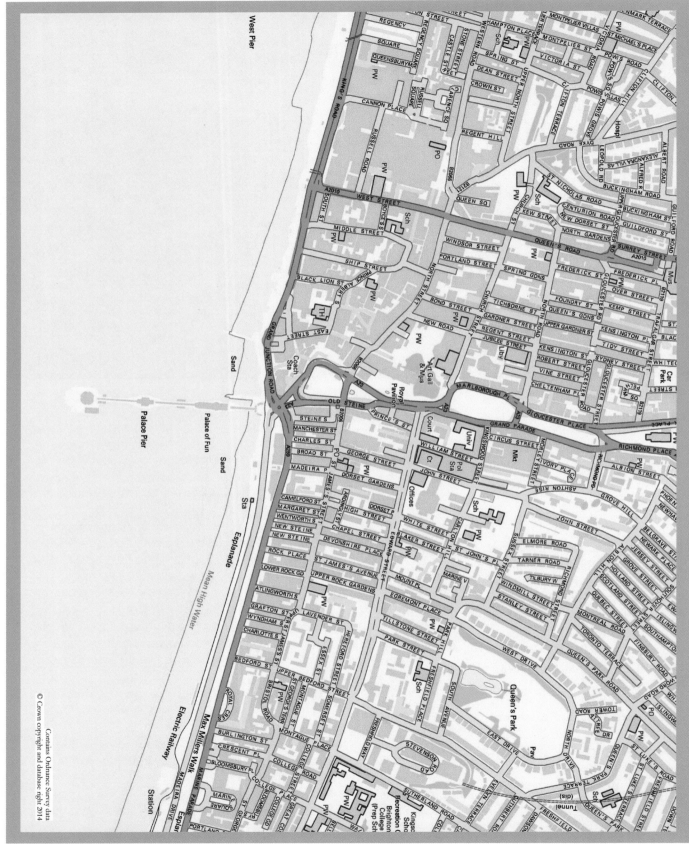

BRIGHTON & HOVE

The first section is about the kid friendly places to go in Brighton. The city is a great place for children, with fantastic parks, interesting museums, cinemas and events.

Take a stroll on the seafront, explore the bohemian shops and cafes around the Lanes and North Laines or have a picnic at the lawn outside the Royal Pavilion. There are handy kids play areas right on the seafront at the Peter Pan playground or King's Road. Queen's park on the hill above Hanover is also very popular.

If it is raining, you could see a movie at the reduced price Saturday morning cinemas. There are five theatres, three cinemas and plenty of indoor play centres so there is always something to do.

There are so many restaurants and cafes, that there are plenty of child friendly places to eat out. In summer, paddle about in the seafront pools. Or take the historic Volks Railway along the beach to find crabs and sealife rock pooling under the cliffs at Rottingdean. Or head to the Sealife Centre at Palace Pier, walk to Hove past the Old Penny Arcade and cafes.

There is good local transport so it is relatively easy to get around. The train runs frequently between Hove, Brighton, Lewes, Eastbourne and London. Buses are frequent, have low floors and buggy access. Cycling or walking you can go for miles along the seafront or in the South Downs.

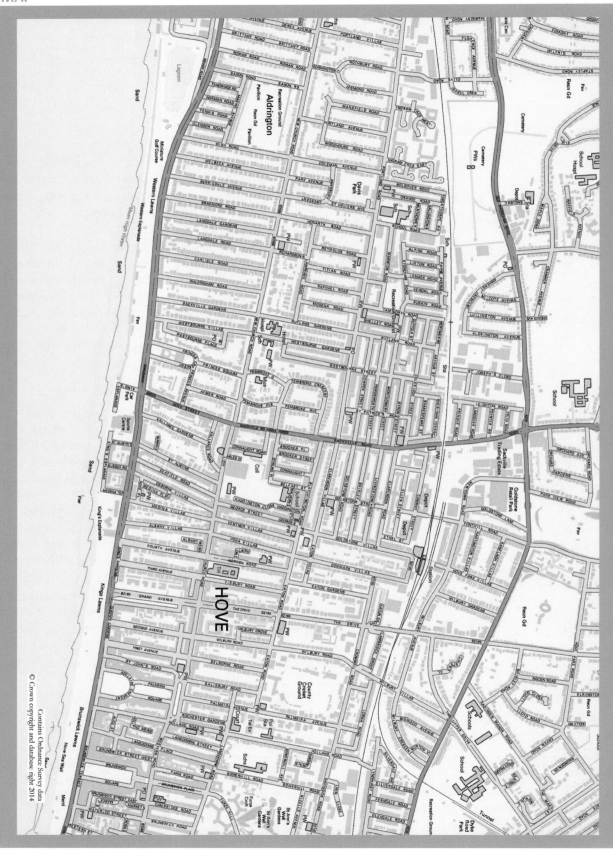

BRIGHTON & HOVE DAYS OUT

Brighton Beach

Brighton is defined by the sea and the pebbly beach. It is fun and hot in the summer, packed full of people. In the winter the crashing waves and moody skies have a quieter charm. Kids love to pick up pebbles and throw them in the water. The sea is just step down from the promenade or through an underground tunnel from West Street. There are also lifeguards who can help with finding lost children and administering first aid.

The Palace Pier section of the beach has been awarded blue flag status. The whole area has a lively feel in the summer, which has always attracted the crowds. During a heatwave in October 2011, 200,000 tourists visited in a single weekend and spent about £5 million.

Brighton Pier

Madeira Drive, Brighton, BN2 1TW
www.brightonpier.co.uk
Known locally as the Palace Pier. The Victorians thought that the sea air was good for health, and so piers were built all over England. This is the only remaining Pier in Brighton, after the West Pier has crumbled into the sea. It is much longer than you think, and very refreshing to take a stroll and look back at the rows or Regency houses and hotels. It has fun fair rides, traditional kids rides, candy floss and a Helter Skelter.

Brighton Royal Pavilion

4/5 Pavilion Buildings, Brighton BN1 1EE
Tel: 03000 290900
www.royalpavilion.org.uk
The Prince Regent was eccentric and decadent. He had the Royal Pavilion built by John 'Marble Arch' Nash in 1823. The inside is even more ornate and excessive, full of a jumble of Chinese and Indian styles. See the mock Bamboo staircase and gilded dragons. There are guided tours especially for children. This is where lavish parties and balls were held by the Prince Regent. Free entrance for children living in Brighton and Hove, adults half price (proof of address must be supplied)

Brighton Wheel

Daltons Bastion, Madeira Drive, Brighton, BN2 1TB
You can see the beach, the sea and Brighton from high up. Standard

capsules: up to six adults and two children.

Volks Electric Railway

The world's oldest operating electric railway. It travels for just over a mile, stopping at the aquarium and the Peter Pan playground.

Peter Pans Adventure Golf

Relatively easy 18 holes with half pipe tunnel, slopes and drop through's. It is next the Peter Pan Playground and the beach.

Brighton Sea Life Centre

Marine Parade, BN2 1TB
Tel: 01273 604234
www.visitsealife.com/brighton
One of Brighton's main attractions. Stand in awe of the sharks, Lulu the giant turtle and tropical reefs. There are seahorses and jellyfish. There is an interactive rock pool where you can touch starfish and crabs. There is over 150 creatures. It is also the world's oldest

Did you know?

- The population of Brighton is 273,400 and Sussex is 1.6 million.
- Brighton has been nicknamed 'The Queen of Watering Places' and 'Old Ocean's Bauble' (Poet Horace Smith); 'Doctor Brighton' (Novelist William Makepeace Thackeray)

Sourced from article:
http://en.wikipedia.org/wiki/Brighton

operating aquarium, at 140 years old.
£12.50 (online); £17.50 (on door)
Mon-Fri, Sat, Sun, 10am-5pm Mon-Fri; 10am-6pm Sat-Sun

Brighton Marina

Just off the A259, Brighton, BN2 5UF
Tel: 01273 628627
www.brightonmarina.co.uk
There are a host of things for families to do at Brighton's Marina. There is a cinema complex, tenpin bowling, outdoor rides, restaurants, pubs and shops. Why not hire

bikes and cycle along the seafront? Or simply take a walk along the boardwalk and take in the sea air and watch the boats.

The Chattri

Standean Lane, Patcham, Brighton
www.chattri.org
Chattri means umbrella in Hindi, Punjabi and Urdu. It is a monument dedicated to the Indian Soldiers who died in the First World War. Many came to the area for medical care. The site is the cremation place for Hindu and Sikh soldiers who died of their wounds at the Royal Pavilion Hospital. It was unveiled in 1921 by the then Prince of Wales. You can find it on the South Downs - the 'Chattri & the Windmills' route.

Brighton Treasure Trail

www.treasuretrails.co.uk/sussex/things-to-do-in-Brightonth.html
It starts at Brighton Pier , is 2 miles long and takes 2 hours to complete.
£6.99

Do you know Norfolk beach from your Bedford?

Separated by groynes, the beaches have names! Some are named after hotels, others after the area.

- Eastwards from Hove boundary, they are called **Boundary, Norfolk, Bedford, Metropole, Grand, Centre, King's, Old Ship, Volk's, Albion, Palace Pier, Aquarium, Athina** (where the MS Athina B ran aground), **Paston, Banjo, Duke's, Cliff, Crescent and Black Rock.**
- Cliff Beach is a nudist beach.

Sourced from article:
http://en.wikipedia.org/wiki/Brighton

Beach Playgrounds

King's Road and the Peter Pan Playground are right on the beach, and great fun for the little ones. There are sand pits, water splash fun and a cafe in each.

Please check with each place you want to visit before you go, by phone or website - to avoid disappointment. Opening times, venues and prices can change.

Peter Pan is on the east of the Brighton Palace Pier, you can get theree on foot or by the Volks Railway. Kings Road is on the other side.

FUN FOR FREE

There is a surprising amount of things to do in Brighton and Sussex for free. Of course there are the parks, playgrounds and open spaces. However there are also some brilliant free events, such as the children's parade and those fabulous vintage cars on the London to Brighton run. Or peruse the strange and wonderful objects in the fantastic museums.

Swimming is free for kids at the main indoor pools, and of course the paddling pools in summer can't be beat for sheer exuberant fun. The often forgotten rich resources of our local libraries are not just about free loans of every kids book imaginable. Most local libraries also run story telling sessions for pre school kiddies. For free!

FREE EVENTS
February
Brighton Science Festival
April
Eastbourne Festival
May
Brighton Festival - many of the arts events around town are free
Brighton Children's Parade
Artists Open Houses
Jack in the Green Festival, Hastings
June
Sussex Festival of Nature, Stanmer Park
July
Kite Festival, Stanmer Park
Paddle around the Pier
August
Arundel Festival

Brighton Gay Pride - Preston Park
Brunswick Festival, Brighton
September
Artwave Festival, Lewes
Open Houses Weekend
November
Lewes Bonfire Night -
London to Brighton veteran car run
December
Burning the Clocks, Brighton

MUSEUMS
Booth Museum of Natural History
Brighton Museum & Art Gallery
Fishing Museum
Hove Museum & Art Gallery

STORY TELLING

Various Libraries in Brighton and Sussex and Brighton Jubilee Library.

SWIMMING
Free sessions for under 16s after 3.30pm weekdays and weekends indoor pools at the King Alfred, Prince Regent and St Luke's. Outdoor paddling pools open in the summer, the following are free: Kings Road; Hove Lagoon

THE SOUTH DOWNS
Right on Brighton's doorstep, the South Downs, the rolling hills, views of the sea and walkways can be a great way to spend the day with kids.

Free Table Tennis in the summer.
Brighton Jubilee Library

Brighton beachfront

A long expansive pebble beach and crashing waves. The elegant Regency Buildings are arranged into squares and crescents facing the sea. The lure of the seafront has been an attraction since the days of the Prince Regent. The promenade runs from Rottingdean to Portslade, now with a cycle lane. The seafront has been redeveloped over the years and is now a bustling place, with seaside shops selling Brighton Rock and windmills, cool cafes, art galleries and sculptures. You can play volleyball and basketball right next to the pebbles. To the east side of Brighton Pier is England's oldest electric railway, the Volks Railway. The Fishing Quarter has a museum, modern art trail and Artists' Quarter. At night it turns into a busy nightlife scene, with funky bars and clubs. In the summer there is entertainment, like the open air cinema and music on the beach.

Brighton Marina

This is the place to be if you have a yacht. It also has shopping, an 8-screen cinema, gym, bowling, casino and several quayside bars, restaurants and cafes. Brighton Marina is easily accessible on the number 7 bus, but if you are travelling by car, parking is free.

Hove

Past the Peace Statue on Brighton seafront lies the adjacent town of Hove. It is lined with tall Regency houses and has some beautiful squares like Brunswick Square and Adelaide Crescent. It is a little quieter but just as well served as Brighton with shops, cafes, entertainment and restaurants. Hove was originally a fishing village near

BRIGHTON VILLAGES

North Laines

the King Alfred Centre. Marlborough Court was once the residence of the Duchess of Marlborough, aunt of Winston Churchill.

Brunswick Town

A popular, tranquil area in Hove with gorgeous Regency architecture. Brunswick Square and Brunswick Terrace are well known examples. This was once Wick Farm in the 18th Century. The architect Charles Busby was commissioned to build in the area by Thomas Read Kemp, creator of the successful Kemp Town Estate.

The Lanes

This was once the centre of the fishing town of Brighthelmstone. The Lane's retain many of the old maze of lanes and alleyways. Now it contains luxury shops of jewellery, fashion and design. It contains some of the best restaurants in town. Some of the buildings are 400 year old fishermen cottages. Black Lion Lane was allegedly the escape route of Charles II. 'Quad-

rophenia Alley' is the alley shown in the cult film Quadrophenia and a reminder of the Mods and Rockers who came in droves to Brighton in the 1960s.

North Laine and Cultural Quarter

This is a fun, quirky area of Brighton. There are many independent and over 300 unique shops and cosy cafes. There are design shops, vintage clothes, organic food shops, trendy bric-a-brac and some very cute kid and baby shops.

Kemp Town

Kemp Town is flamboyant, bustling but small enough to feel cosy. Like Hove, it has some beautiful Regency houses in smaller but just as elegant squares. It is here you find the boutique fashionable hotels. Thomas Read Kemp built the Kemp Town estate in the earl 1800s. St James's Street has an eclectic array of cafes and interior design shops. It is here that you'll find some of the best bars and

Old Brighton

- Brighton used to be the ancient settlement of Brighthelmstone, which dates before the Domesday Book (1086). It is a Saxon name, probably meaning village by the sea. It had a population of only 400 people!
- The railway reached the town in 1841 and became very popular as a day trip from London.
- It became popular as a health resort with sea bathing thought to cure a lot of ills in Victorian times.

Sourced from article: http://en.wikipedia.org/wiki/Brighton

pubs in town, as well as the city's thriving gay quarter.'The result is that it became one of the most desirable areas of the town and home to many famous residents from Lewis Carrol to the Sixth Duke of Devonshire.

Hanover

The streets are relatively narrow and quite steep, carrying shopping back is like a gym workout! It has a very strong sense of community. Many families live here, and it is close to the Level and Queen's Park. Some very welcoming pubs, there is even a street and beer festival each year. Famous residents include Sir Rowland Hill, who introduced the Penny Black stamp, who lived in Hanover Terrace. Horace Smith, a writer and poet, lived in Hanover Crescent, where he held parties for literary society.

Seven Dials

This is high up in the hills back from the seafront. The dials are the seven roads that radiate out from the hub. It is again a thriving community, well served by buses and the London Road train station.

The Brighton Walk of Fame

A trail of 100 plaques in Brighton Marina. Discover the colourful characters who have lived and live in the City, from the original party socialite, the Prince Regent to the superstar DJ, Fatboy Slim.

Rottingdean

Rudyard Kipling lived here. You can walk to Rottingdean from Brighton Marina via the undercliff walk, or take the bus. It is a picturesque seaside village that became fashionable in the nineteenth century among artists, writers and pol-

iticians. It has some lovely tea shops.

Churchill Square and Western Road

This is the main, modern quarter. Churchill Square is the indoor shopping centre with all the well known high-street names such as Debenhams. Late night shopping is on Thursday. Western Road is busy with main shops and cafes.

Silicon Beach

- Brighton has a high number of media businesses, and has been referred to as "Silicon Beach". By 2007, over 250 new media business had been founded in Brighton.
- Brighton's largest private sector employer is American Express.
- The tourism industry of the city contributes £380m to the economy and employs 20,000 people.
- In December 2013, Brighton was the third-highest ranked place on the UK Vitality Index Report, which measures the economic strength of towns in the UK.

Sourced from article: http://en.wikipedia.org/wiki/Brighton

Barefoot Café / Bar @ Yellowave

Yellowave Beachsports kids activities in Brighton Yellowave Beach Sports Venue, 299 Madeira Drive, Brighton BN2 1EN
Tel: 01273 672222.
This has a sandy play area for children and good coffee, what more could you want?! It is very popular with toddlers and parents alike. There are sandwiches, soup and snacks too. Open all year round. Summer open weekdays 10am-10pm, Sat & Sun 10am-8pm).

Hove Park Cafe

Hove Park, Park View Road, Hove BN3 7BF, Tel: 01273 727003
A great spot in this lovely park, and nice, honest good food.

Olde Cottage Tea Rooms and Restaurant

The Olde Cottage Tea Rooms and Restaurant, 62-64 High Street, Rottingdean, Brighton, East Sussex BN2 7HF
Tel: 01273 303426
Lovely tearoom in the village of Rottingdean. Originally built in 1589 A.D, it is a very cosy and quaint.

Temptation Cafe

56 Gardner Street, Brighton, BN1 1UN
Tel: 01273 673045
www.brightontemptation.com
Independent cafe specialising in local food. Good children's menu, such as chicken pieces with couscous. My favourite is the 'Baby Grazing Platter' for toddlers.

There are some great places to eat in Brighton, from breakfast cafes to upmarket restaurants. Many of the restaurants and cafes are welcoming of children. Here is a persoanl selection, however there are many more. Brighton has about 400 restaurants more per head than anywhere else outside London.

Cafes & Tea Shops

Big Beach Cafe

Hove Lagoon, Kingsway,
Hove BN3 4LX
Tel: 01273 911080
bigbeachcafe.com

Another great location next to Hove Lagoon, with outdoor seating too. It has good solid kids food such as hot dogs, chips, cakes and organic ice cream. This is Norman Cook's (aka Fat Boy Slim's) cafe and previously owned by Heather Mills.
Open: 10am - 6pm

Bucket and Spade beach cafe

26-28 Kings Arches, Brighton BN1 2LN
Tel: 01273 220222
On the seafront, next to the West Pier paddling pool / playground. All home made, freshly cooked food, very child friendly, with a healthy menu for children!

Burgers & Diners

Gourmet Burger Kitchen
44-47 Gardner Street, Brighton BN1 1UN
 Tel: 01273 685895
www.gbk.co.uk
Very big, juicy taster burgers that feel more wholesome than the chains.

Giraffe
15 North Road, Brighton BN1 1YA,
Tel: 01273 688 885
Close to the Jubilee Library, with a kids menu and great fruit smoothies.

Las Iguanas
7 Jubilee Street, Brighton BN1 1GE,
Tel: 01273 573 550
www.iguanas.co.uk
They have a good children's selection and some very tasty fare.

Lucky Beach
Kings Road arches
http://luckybeach.co.uk
One of the nicer places to get burgers on the beach. The burgers are from £5.95 and you can have luxury mayo.

Woodies Diner
366 Kingsway, Hove BN3 4QT
Tel: 01273 430300
www.woodiesdiner.com
A nice 1950s style diner, with a jukebox and vintage surfboards. Great burgers and a children's menu.

Fish & Chips

Bankers Fish Restaurant
116a Western Road, Brighton BN1 2AB
Tel: 01273 328267 / 820111

Award winning fish restaurant. They have a children's menu and activity packs.
Open: 11:30am-10pm

Bardsley's Fish and Chip Shop
Baker Street, Brighton
Tel: 01273 681256
www.bardsleys-fishandchips.co.uk
The place to go for quality fish and chips. There's nothing like eating chips by the sea after a wander around the beach or the town.

Ice Cream

Boho Gelato
6 Pool Valley, Brighton BN1 1NJ
Tel: 01273 727205
This traditional Italian ice cream parlour with some brilliant flavours, from violet to vanilla, apple to avocado.

Scoop and Crumb
5 East Street, Brighton, BN1 1HP
Tel: 01273 202563
Homemade ice-creams made on the premises using natural ingredients, 50 different ice cream sundaes to choose from, as well as waffles, shakes, the largest selection of hot dogs in the city.

Defies a Label

Alfresco
26 Kings Road Arches, Brighton, East Sussex BN1 2LN,
Tel: 01273 206 523
www.alfresco-brighton.co.uk
A a great location, by the West Pier. It has good views. It is at the pricier end, with crab cakes, tiger prawns, pasta and pizzas.

Bom-Bane
24 George St, Brighton BN2 1RH
Tel: 01273 606400
Described as quirky and friendly, with a mixture of English and Belgian. An eclectic place.

Plateau
1 Bartholomews, Brighton BN1 1HG
Tel: 01273 733 085
www.plateaubrighton.co.uk
For a more upmarket treat, a local independent wine bar and restaurant. It has a bites menu where everyone can share tasters.

Thewitchez Photo Design Cafe Bar
16 Marine Parade,
Brighton BN2 7TL
Tel: 01273 673652
www.thewitchez-cafe.co.uk
Open every day until late. Home made pizza, apple half moons, polish sausages. It has has photographic studio. Evenings have silent movies.

Tin Drum (Hove)
10 Victoria Grove, Second Avenue, Hove BN3 2LJ, Tel: 01273 747755
www.tindrum.co.uk
All three bars and restaurants are child friendly. The Hove Tin Drum has a large outside area and the food is produced on the owners farm.

Italian

Al Duomo
7 Pavilion Buildings, Brighton, BN1 1EE, Tel: 07710 161562

www.alduomo.co.uk
A very popular Italian restaurant, and an easy place to take the kids. They have a kids pack with colouring.

Carluccios

Italian
Jubilee Street, Brighton BN1 1GE
Tel: 01273 690493
www.carluccios.com
A popular Italian restaurant that is great with kids and very central.

Donatello

1-3 Brighton Place, The Lanes, Brighton BN1 1HJ
Tel: 01273 775477
www.donatello.co.uk
A family friendly Italian restaurant centrally located in the Lanes. Activity colouring packs for the kids.

Frankie & Benny's

3 The Waterfront, Brighton BN2 5WB
Tel: 01273 688450
It has a varied kids and juniors menu and organic baby food. All the main kid staples are catered for like spaghetti bolognaise, bananas and custard, burgers and ice-cream. Birthday parties can be pre-booked.
Hours: Mon - Sat:: 09:00-23:00, Sun: 09:00-22.30

Pinocchio

22 New Road, Brighton, BN1 1UF
Tel: 01273 677 676
www.pinoccio.co.uk
This Italian restaurant is family friendly and family run! It is very popular with Brighton residents, as well as visitors. It serves fresh Italian food.

Pizza Express

22 Prince Albert Street, Brighton, BN1 1HF
Tel: 01273 323 205
107 Church Road, Hove, BN3 2AF
Tel: 01273 770 093
www.pizzaexpress.co.uk
For tasty pizzas and salads, you are never far away from a Pizza Express. Their set price Piccolo menu includes dough balls and Bambinoccino.

Pizza Hut

Brighton Marina, Brighton, BN2 5WA
Tel: 01273 622233
www.pizzahut.co.uk/pizza-brighton
Another family restaurant that can be reasonable and reliable, although as a chain they don't have the individual flair of an independent place. However they do a good kids menu.

Pablo's

36 Ship Street, Brighton BN1 1AB
Tel: 01273 208123
Budget friendly Italian pizzeria in central Brighton, it is maybe not the highest quality in the city but it is cheerful and reasonable.

Japanese

Moshi Moshi

Opticon, Bartholomew Square, Brighton BN1 1JS
Tel: 01273 719195
www.moshibrighton.co.uk
Gorgeous tasting Japanese food and sushi, with fresh seasonal ingredients. A bit of a treat. Brighton's original and favourite Japanese restaurant, known for its handmade sushi, authentic Japanese hot dishes.

Thai, Indian, Moroccan

Chilli Pickle Bistro

MyHotel, 17 Jubilee Street, Brighton BN1 1GE
Tel: 01273 900383
www.thechillipickle.com
Nice Indian Bistro with a street menu, accommodating with children.

Mascara

101 Western Road, Brighton BN1 2AA
Tel: 01273278185
www.mascara-restaurant.co.uk
A friendly Moroccan restaurant.
Open: 5pm til late. Book in advance for Friday/Sat nights.

Pho

12 Black Lion Street, Brighton, Brighton, BN1 1ND
Tel: 01273 202403
info@phocafe.co.uk
www.phocafe.co.uk
Nice fresh noodle soups and tasty noodle dishes. They have smaller versions of the adult dishes for kids.

Sabai Thai Gastrobar

165-169 Princes House, Princes Place BN1 1EA
Tel: 01273773030
bookings@sabaibrighton.co.uk
www.sabaibrighton.co.uk
Bronze award winner 2014 for best family dining at Brighton and Hove Food and Drink Awards. Try the Pad Thai or Fried Rice, and sit on the Thai cushions to eat.

Roast Dinners

Gingerman

21A Norfolk Square, Brighton BN1 2PD
It is fairly small, but serves lovely food. The roast dinner is great, a huge chunk of roast beef, served pink with perfect roasties and yorkshire pudding.

Vegetarian

Food For Friends

Vegetarian
17-18 Prince Albert Street, BN1 1HF
Tel: 01273 202310
www.foodforfriends.com
Another great vegetarian restaurant with some inventive meals to tempt the tastebuds.

Terre a Terre

Vegetarian
71 East Street, BN1 1HQ
Tel: 01273 729051
www.terreaterre.co.uk
A well established vegetarian restaurant that has a loyal following. Well prepared and thoughtful dishes.

Picnics

Brighton has many green lawned, grassy spaces that can be a perfect spot for picnics. Here are a few ideas:

- Only take what you can carry easily if you are going on foot or cycling. It sounds obvious but it's easy to be weighed down.

- Sandwich fillings: marmite & cheese, tuna, ham, jam. Crackers, carrot sticks, dips, crisps, small slices of pizza. Fruit juice in cartons and water.

- Children can get dehydrated in the sun so make sure you have plenty to drink.

- Wipes, plastic bags for rubbish, sun hats & cream, picnic blanket.

- Games like frisbee, football, or exploring with a magnifying glass to look at insects.

- Check the weather. Bring waterproofs in case.

Top picnic spots in Sussex

- Arundel Castle
- Cuckmere Haven
- Ditchling Beacon
- Grange Gardens, Lewes
- Kingley Vale, West Stoke, Chichester
- Preston Park or Queen's Park, Brighton
- Stanmer Park

PARKS, PLAYGROUNDS & GREEN SPACES

Brighton has lots of playgrounds, some right on the beach. In Hove Laggon there is a sandpit, Kings Road there are climbing frames, sand and a big paddling pool. In Peter Pan playground you can have a drink and snack at the cafe, the park is completely enclosed and you get get there by the Volks Railway.

Preston Park, Hove Park and Queen's Pard are all big with lots of facilities for families. Preston and Hove Parks each have excellent sports facilities such as football, tennis and basketball courts.

There are wilder areas such as East Brighton Park near Sheepcote Valley, a nature reserve. Hollingbury is a historic place, with a strategic viewpoint over Brighton and the Downs. It was thought to have been a promiment site for early Celtic people, however now it is a great place to walk and enjoy the woods.

Recreation and Playgrounds

Blakers Park
Cleveland Road, Brighton, BN1 6FF
www.blakerspark.org.uk
A small park, which manages to pack in tennis courts, a cafe and playground. It has a distinctive Victorian clocktower.

Dyke Road Park
Dyke Road, Brighton
This has a small playground area and is very close to the Booth Museum of Natural History. This park has paths winding around shrubs and borders. It has a raised terraced cafe with good views.

Easthill Park
Trafalgar Road, Portslade
This has a beautiful walled garden, and includes the War Memorial.

East Brighton Park
Nr Sheepcote Valley, Brighton, BN2 5TS
A sense of openness in this big expanse of grass. The nature reserve Sheepcote Valley is nearby.

Hollingbury Park and Woods
Ditchling Rd, Brighton, BN1 7HS
One of my favourite parks, high up over the Hollingbury and Hollingdean community. It has walks through the woods and expanses of open space. There is a large new playground with picnic tables.

Hove Lagoon
Kingsway, Hove BN3 4LX
As well as the lagoon, there is a playground, a sandpit, a paddling pool and toilet. There are two lagoons here. The biggest is used by the Hove Lagoon Watersports.

Hove Park
Parkview Road, Hove BN3 7BF
www.brighton-hove.gov.uk/content/leisure-and-libraries/parks-and-green-spaces/hove-park
A big park with plenty of space to run around, let off steam or walk with a buggy. 40 acres or grass, trees, flowers and sports facilities. It also has a playground, toilets and cafe. Oh and a miniature steam railway! It has a Fingermaze, football pitches, tennis & basketball courts and bowling greens. This is a large and pretty park. It has a lovely café. This has sports pitches and facilities, an adventure playground, a climbing boulder and miniature railway. There is also a strangely named Goldstone and Fingermaze.

Kings Road Playground
Right on the seafront. This has sand and climbing frames, and equipment especially for children under 7 years old. There's a huge old fashioned paddling pool. It's great for a sunny day. There is also a café, and deck chairs for hire.

Queens Park
South Avenue, Brighton BN2 0BP

and Hanover, this lovely park has a playground, a cafe, toilets, tennis courts, a pond and a wildlife garden. The playground has a sandpit, children and toddler area. It is a very popular place with families. This park has a lake with a fountain and ducks to feed, a playground with separate children and toddler areas, a sandpit, a wildlife garden and a scented garden. There are also toilets and a cafe.

Peter Pan's Playground
Madeira Drive, Brighton
This is a fully enclosed adventure playground by the seafront, with water spouts. It is especially suitable for young children. It has an open air cafe, toilets and its own train stop on the Volks Electric Railway.

Preston Park
Preston Road, Brighton BN1 6HL
www.brighton-hove.gov.uk
This is a beautiful and historic park. The largest urban park in the city. Plenty of sports activities for kids, and you can also relax and enjoy the gardens or the cafes. It has a great children's adventure playground, two cafes, toilets, football & cricket pitches, basket ball & tennis courts. It has a rose garden, a 1920s Rotunda tea pavilion and a romantic walled garden. The park is lovely for a sedate walk or for family sports activities. It even has a velodrome.

Saunders Park
Saunders Park View, Lewes Road, Brighton, East Sussex BN2 4AY
On the Lewes Road near the Vogue Gyratory System. It is opposite the Lewes Bus Garage. It has a refurbished Play Area, Toddler playground and paddling pool.

St Ann's Well Gardens
Somerhill Road, Hove BN3 1RP
This is in Hove near the seafront, with gardens and trees, it is a haven from a day out shopping or a break from sightseeing. There is a garden café, toilets and a fish pond. Tennis courts, a bowling green and a sensory garden.

Stanmer Park
Moulsecoomb/Bevendean
Lewes Road, Brighton, BN1 9SE
This is a fantastic place to explore, a little like going back in time. There park is the countryside around Stanmer village, with Stanmer House, the gardens, Stanmer Organics/Earthship, the church and woods above the valley. There is a nice tearoom.

The woodlands are great to explore with the kids, and the open countryside in the valley is full of history. You could spend a summers day here with a picnic, explore the church and the Downs.

Stoneham Park
This has a playground and a community run café. It has some shaded areas for and a rock garden area too.

The Level
The Level, Ditchling Road, Brighton BN1 4ZN
One of the most central spaces, just behind St Peters Church and it has been renovated in recent years to become a great public space, particularly for kids and teenagers. It has a good playground, water features, a nice little cafe kiosk and a skateboard ramp.

Wild Park
Lewes Rd, Brighton BN1 9JS
This is Brighton & Hove's largest local nature reserve. A great space for walking. You see local wildlife; butterflies, birds and insects. It also has wonderful views, and a large amount of woodland. A good place to spot different kinds of trees, and kick about autumn leaves.

Withdean Park
London Road, Brighton
This is a semi wild large park with lovely views of the Downs. It has woodland on the north and east borders, and is popular with dog walkers.

Queen's Park *via Wikimedia Commons*

What to do When it's Pouring Outside

It's raining outside but the little ones are getting restless. What is there to do?

There are some great museums in Brighton, most of them free. From the old photographs of fishermen in the Fishing Museum to a huge range of performance, pottery and art at the Brighton or Hove Museums of Art.

There are three good local cinemas; **Cineworld**, the Duke of Yorks and the **Odeon** which all have special children showings. And if you fancy letting the kids run around and let off steam, there are soft play areas, or the King Al-fred or the Prince Regent swimming pools and leisure centres.

Or you can put on the raincoats and wellies and let the kids splash in puddles!

Cinemas

Cineworld
Brighton Marina, Brighton BN2 5UF
Tel: 0871 200 2000
www.cineworld.co.uk/cinemas/3
Multi screen cinema complex. At 10am on Saturday mornings, Cineworld cinema at Brighton Marina offers 2-3 special "Movies for Juniors" screenings with pre-show entertainment (colouring competition) for younger customers.

Duke of Yorks Cinema
Preston Circus, Brighton, BN1 4NA
Tel: 0871 704 2056
www.picturehouses.co.uk/cinema/Duke_Of_Yorks
Established in 1910, the Duke of Yorks has been operating as an arts cinema since 1981. It has a Kids club on Saturdays, starting at 10.30am, and also hosts children's parties. The Big

Scream on Wednesdays at 11am is a screening for parents with babies under one year.

The Odeon Cinema
Kingswest, West Street, Brighton BN1 2RE
Tel: 0871 22 44 007
www.odeon.co.uk/fanatic/film_times/s71/Brighton/
Multi screen cinema complex in the centre of Brighton. The Kids screenings are every Saturday and Sunday mornings at pocket money prices.

Soft Play Centres

Funplex
The Hyde Business Park, Auckland Drive, Bevendean, Brighton BN2 4JE
Tel: 01273 690888
www.funplex.co.uk
A 3 level playframe which includes a 4 lane astra slide, a softball cannon arena and a maze area. Toddler section with a 2 level playframe with its own slide, a ball pool and a large baby area. £3.95/ £5.25 (under 4); £4.75/ £5.75 (over 4)
Mon-Fri, Sat, Sun, 10am-6pm daily

Jump for Joy
Tarner Children's Centre, Ivory Place, Brighton BN2 9QE
Tel and Booking: 01273
play activity group for children under 5 (term time only). Fridays, 10-10.45 & 11-11.45am. Free.

Monkey Bizness Indoor Play Centre
Unit 27, Cliffe Industrial Estate, Lewes BN8 6JL

Tel: 08458 739 645
Indoor soft play centre in Lewes, offering three different play frames to accommodate different ages from 0-2's, 2-5's and 5-12's. It has an area for crawling children.

Westows
School Road, Hove, BN3 5HX
Tel: 01273 721338
www.westows.com
Indoor play centre for children, large 2 level soft play area and a separate soft play area for under 4s. 2 indoor football pitches with bouncy castle and play toys. £4 (under 4); £4.40 (5 and over); Babies/ adults free.

Olympos (The Triangle)
The Triangle, Triangle Way, Burgess Hill, Brighton RH15 8WA
Tel: 01444 876001
www.olymposcentres.co.uk
Softplay for the under 8s. It has a 25m indoor pool, outdoor pool, flumes, watersprays, waterfalls and rapids.

Story Telling

Jubilee Library
Jubilee Street, Brighton BN1 1GE
Tel: 01273 290800
www.brighton-hove.gov.uk/jubilee-library

Jubilee Library in Brighton

The central library for Brighton and Hove, this library has won 14 awards since opening. This and several of the local libraries run free sessions for babies and toddlers during term time.

The storytimes sessions are usually half an hour and are a really nice way of introducing your child to reading in a social way. Please see more details on page

Brighton in the Movies
Brighton featured in a number of popular movies including Brighton Rock (2010 and 1947), Quadrophenia (1979), The End of the Affair (1999), MirrorMask (2005), Angus, Thongs and Perfect Snogging (2008), The Young Victoria (2009), and The Boat that Rocked (2009).

Sourced from article: http://en.wikipedia.org/wiki/List_o f_films_set_in_Brighton

Making Fairy Cakes

Staying Inside
What do you do if you are stuck inside?

Painting and Getting Messy
Let their creative streaks run wild with a good paint session, with brushes, fingers or making shapes out of potatoes.

Camping Indoors
Use blankets, chairs and tables or sofas and torches and let them make a den.

Chill Out Time
A good DVD or children's program can help everyone to relax after a busy day.

Make a Box House/Car/Boat
Any huge boxes are worth saving. You can cut out windows and doors or eye holes.

Dressing Up
A box of odd rags and outfits.

Playing in the Sink
Let them play with their water toys.

Little Chefs
There are lots of great children's cookbooks or ideas online, to make pizzas, cakes, cookies or lemonade.

MUSEUMS

Booth Museum of Natural History

194 Dyke Road, Brighton BN1 5AA
Tel: 03000 290900
www.brighton-hove-rpml.org.uk
British birds, butterflies, skeletons, dinosaur bones and a whale are housed here. The Victorian ornithologist Edward Booth is the original (Closed 12 – 1.15pm), Sun 2 – 5pm Closed Thu (open on Bank Holiday Mondays) Free admisssion

Brighton Toy and Model Museum

52-55 Trafalgar Street, BN1 4EB
Tel: 01273 749494
www.brightontoymuseum.co.uk
This is a small place, you could easily miss it! It is nestled under the arches of the station, at the top of Trafalgar Street. It has some slightly strange puppets, and old dolls furniture, train sets and toys. There are over 10,000 toys and models on display. Adults £4.50; child £3.50

Brighton Royal Pavilion

4/5 Pavilion Buildings, Brighton BN1 1EE
Tel: 03000 290900
www.royalpavilion.org.uk
The Prince Regent was eccentric and decadent. He had the Royal Pavilion built by John 'Marble Arch' Nash in 1823. The inside is even more ornate and excessive, full of a jumble of Chinese and Indian styles. See the mock Bamboo staircase and gilded dragons. There are guided tours especially for children. This is where lavish parties and balls were held by the Prince Regent. Free entrance for children living in Brighton and Hove, adults half price (proof of address must be supplied)
Open daily Apr-Sep 9.30am –5.45pm (last admission 5pm) Oct-Mar 10am – 5.15pm (last admission 4.30pm) Admission fee payable.

Brighton Museum & Art Gallery

Royal Pavilion Gardens, Brighton, BN1 1EE
Tel: 03000 290900
www.brighton-hove
rpml.org.uk/museums
It is a great place, full of quirky treasures and interactive displays for all the family. It has a 20th Century Decorative Art & Design gallery, The Performance gallery, Mr Willett's Popular Pottery gallery and learn about the rich and colourful history of Brighton. It has an Indian gateway and a big craft collection. Open Tue – Sun 10am – 5pm, Closed Mon (except Bank Holidays 10am – 5pm)
Free entrance.

Fishing Museum

201 King's Road Arches, BN1 1NB
Tel: 01273 723064
www.brightonfishingmuseum.org.uk
Brighton was originally a fishing village, and the smell of fish would have permeated the streets all around the town. This is a volunteer run museum which has some of the fishing history and photographs of the place. There are also restored traditional Sussex clinker boats. It is well worth a visit. Free admission.

Hove Museum & Art Gallery

19 New Church Road, Hove, BN3 4AB
Tel: 03000 290900
www.brighton-hove
rpml.org.uk/Museums

A good place to take the kids. It has an assortment of toys on display in the Wizard's Attic. There is a magical toy treasure chest, along with dolls, teddy bears, mechanical toys, toy trains and dolls houses, rocking horses and tricycles from history. The film gallery shows the pioneering Hove film-makers of the 1890s and 1900s. Learn about the history of Hove, from prehistoric times. There are prints and paintings, and a contemporary Craft Gallery.
Open Mon, Tue, Thu, Fri & Sat ,10am –5pm, Sun 2 – 5pm. Closed Wed (open on Bank Holiday Mondays) Free admission.

Mechanical Memories

250C King's Road Arches, BN1 1NB
www.mechanicalmemoriesmuseum.co.uk
This is a working museum, full of vintage slot machines. You can buy big old fashioned pennies and try fortune tellers, horse racing or spooky ghosts. Open 12-6pm weekends and school holidays only. Free entry but you'll probably want to buy some old pennies.

Old Police Cells Museum

Town Hall, Bartholomew Square, Brighton BN1 1JA
01273 291052
www.oldpolicecellsmuseum.org.uk
For any little budding policemen, this museum has all you need to know about the force in Brighton. charts the history of policing in Brighton. You can even have a look into the cells. There are tales of the mods and rockers, a murdered chief constable and more.
Open April until October. Access is only by pre-booked guided tours at 10.30 am when the museum is open. To book your place, please telephone, in advance, Brighton Town Hall Reception on 01273 291052.

Preston Manor

Preston Drove, Brighton, BN1 6SD
Tel: 03000 290900
www.virtualmuseum.info

An Edwardian home which belonged to the Stanford family for over 200 years. It has original furniture, ceramics and locks. Free entrance for local residents (with proof of address). See the servants' quarters and hall, butlers' pantry, boot hall, kitchen, head housemaids' and personal maids' rooms can all be seen, together with a period walled garden and family pets graveyard.
Please note: Closed: 1 October-31 March.
Open Apr-Sep, Tue-Fri 10am – 5pm,
Sun 2 – 5pm (last admission 4.15pm) Closed Mon (including Bank Holidays) & Sat .
Admission fee payable

Preston Manor via Wikimedia Commons

THEATRES

Emporium Theatre
88 London Road, Brighton
http://emporiumbrighton.com
Brighton's only professional producing theatre. It has a cafe, bar and mini exhibition area.

Komedia
44-47 Gardner Street,
Brighton BN1 1UN
Tel: 0845 293 8480/01273 647100
www.komedia.co.uk
This is a great place for alternative nights out. It includes children's theatre and is open during the day as a café. It has been voted "Best Family Friendly Theatre in the South". Look out for the Cool Music for Cool Kids discos, 0-8 yrs; a Comedy Club 4 Kids (over 6's); & Sundae Club.

The New Venture Theatre
Bedford Place, Brighton BN1 2PT
Tel: 01273 808353
www.newventure.org.uk
This has been going for over 50 years. It puts on amateur productions and showcases experimental work too. The theatre is closed awaiting refurbishment.

The Dome
Church Street, Brighton BN1
Box Office: 01273 709709
www.brightondome.org
Brighton Dome is an historic venue on the Royal Pavilion estate, made up of three main spaces: the Concert Hall, Corn Exchange and Studio Theatre. This has many varied performances, workshops and events, with many children's activities.

Theatre Royal
New Road, Brighton BN1 1SD
Box Office: 08448 717 650
www.ambassadortickets.com/Theatre-Royal-Brighton
The Theatre Royal is a very popular live entertainment venue in Brighton. It is a Grade II listed building is one of the oldest working theatres in the country.

Ropetackle Arts Centre - Shoreham
Little High Street, Shoreham-By-Sea, BN43 5EG
This is a purpose built community-run arts venue just outside of Brighton in Shoreham-by-Sea.

MAX MILLER
1894 --- 1963

LIBRARIES

Libraries are a great free resource. They all have good children's sections, with books available for kids from babies, to toddlers teenagers. There are also DVD rentals available, and access to computers.

The free music and rhyme sessions for pre-school children and their parents or carers are a good way to introduce your child to books. They are short enough not to demand too much from kids and can be a nice way of getting to know other parents.

You don't need to book these sessions but if there are too many children there may be a limit. The local libraries also provide a Baby Boogie CD that can be used at home. There are also have Dads' Baby Boogie sessions once a month in Jubilee Library.

Brighton & Hove Libraries

Coldean Library
Library Court, 24 Beatty Avenue, Brighton, BN1 9EW
Tel: 01273 296902

Hangleton Library
West Way, Hangleton Hove BN3 8LD Tel: 01273 296904

Hollingbury Library
Carden Hill Hollingbury BN1 8DA
Tel: 01273 296908

Hove Library
182-186 Church Road, Hove, BN3 2EG
Tel: 01273 296937

Jubilee Library
Jubilee Street, Brighton BN1 1GE
Tel: 01273 290800
The central library for Brighton and Hove, this library has won 14 awards since opening.

Mile Oak Library

Chalky Road, Mile Oak, Portslade, BN41 2WS Tel: 01273 296916

Moulsecoomb Library
The Highway, Moulsecoomb, BN2 4PA
Tel: 01273 296910

Patcham Library
Ladies Mile Road, Patcham, Brighton BN1 8TA
Tel: 01273 296912

Portslade Library
223 Old Shoreham Road, Portslade BN41 1XR
Tel: 01273 296914

Rottingdean Library
The Grange, Rottingdean, Brighton BN2 7HA
Tel: 01273 296918

Lewes Library

Styles Field, Friars Walk, Lewes BN7 2LZ

Tel: 0345 60 80 196
www.eastsussex.gov.uk/libra
ries/find/default.aspx

Rhymetime first Tuesday of every month 10.30am to 11am. Storytime every Monday 2pm to 2.30pm

Story and Rhyme times

(Correct at time of print, 2014. Please check before attending in case they have changed). For further information: www.citylibraries.info

Hangleton Library - fourth Thursday of the month starting 23 October 10.15am-10.45am

Hollingbury Library - second Thursday of the month starting 9 October 10.15am-10.45am

Hove Library - second and fourth Thursday of the month starting 9 October 2.15pm-2.45pm

Jubilee Library - alternate Mondays starting 6 October 10.15-10.45 am

Patcham Library - second Tuesday of the month starting 11 November 10.15am-10.45am

Portslade Library - third Tuesday of the month starting 21 October 10.15am-10.45am

Saltdean Library - first Tuesday of the month starting 7 October 2.15pm-2.45pm

Westdene Library - third Tuesday of the month starting 21 October 2.15pm-2.45pm

Whitehawk Library - first Tuesday of the month starting 7 October 10.15am-10.45am

Top Reads for Kids

There are some books that are magical for children and thought provoking for teenagers, in a way that is not quite the same as reading it as an adult. These are some of my personal favourites, I'm sure that you will have your own.

The Very Hungry Caterpillar by Eric Carle
In almost every format that you can think of now, big books, small books, ones that you can wriggle your fingers through. A classic toddlers book.

Guess How Much I Love You by Sam McBratney
Very sweet tale that doesn't seem to get stale.

The Hobbit J R R Tolkien
I read this as a teenager and it is such a vivid world it completely takes your imagination away.

Green Eggs and Ham by Dr. Seuss
Fun and quirky book.

Where the Wild Things Are by Maurice Sendak
There's something about this tale that is timeless. A great book.

The Lion, the Witch and the Wardrobe by C S Lewis
Another great book for an older child, full of fantasy and adventure.

The Magic Faraway Tree by Enid Blyton
I used to love this book as a child. Different worlds come to the magic tree, where the children meet Silky, Moon Face and the Saucepan Man.

Chicka Chicka Boom Boom by Bill Martin
Rhyming book full of lively images as the letters of the alphabet have an adventure.

Wonder by R. J. Palacio
August Pullman was born with a facial difference, and now wants to be treated as an ordinary boy.

The Little Prince by Antoine de Saint-Exupéry
He falls to earth, full of tales of other planets. A sweet tale.

James and the Giant Peach by Roald Dahl
These are all good books from Roald Dahl. This is one of the major classics, about the tale of small creatures riding in a Giant Peach. A fantastic story.

Diary of a Wimpy Kid by Jeff Kinney
My son loved all of these books. Great to get a child into reading if they are not very bookish.

Winnie the Pooh by A A Milne
You can even visit Ashford Forest, where Winnie the Pooh was said to live in 100 acre wood. A classic tale.

The Day the Crayons Quit by Oliver Jeffers
Crayons have feelings too! A funny tale about crayons from a best selling author.

The Just So Stories by Rudyard Kipling
I think these are marvellous now as they were then. How did the leopard get his spots? It's more fun that these are imaginative answers and not facts.

Captain Underpants by Dav Pilkey
Again, my son would laugh out loud to these tales. Easy to read novels and a lot of irreverent fun.

Harry Potter and the Philosopher's Stone by J K Rowling
To be honest I've never read any of these but my kids, my friends kids... everyone loves them!

Comics:

Marvel Adventures: The Avengers - The characters and stories are well developed and the stories are good.

The Phoenix: A regular comic for 6-12 year olds with no ads, just good fun stories.

Brighton Tours

As a busy seaside town, there are a few city tours to choose from. The following are just a some of those on offer:

Earthship Brighton

www.lowcarbon.co.uk/tours
The Low Carbon Trust offers tours of Earthship Brighton. There are regular tours that are open to anybody. Please note that regular tours do not need to be booked in advance. The charge for individuals on our regular tours is £5 per person and children are welcome. Children under 10 are free.

Brighton Sewer Tours

www.sewertours.southernwater.co.uk
Explore the Victorian narrow, white-washed corridors and up and down metal ladders. Suitable for over 11 years, wear sensible dress. Be warned, ironically, there are no public conveniences! All visits must be pre-booked. Weather permitting, tours take place between May and September. During May, tours are at 6.30pm on Tuesdays and Thursdays and at 9.30am and 11am on Saturdays. From June to September, tours take place at 6.30pm on Wednesdays and 9.30am and 11am on Saturdays.
2013 Prices: £12 per adult and £6 for 11 to 16 year olds.

Brighton Chocolate Walking Tour

by Chocolate Ecstasy Tours
Meeting Point: Outside 103 Gloucester Road, Brighton BN1 4AP
Tel: 0203 4321 306
www.chocolateecstasytours.com
Tours must be booked online in advance. Taste luxury chocolates, and sea-salted caramels. A tour for any chocolate lovers. Price: £33

Curious About Brighton?

robert@curiousabout.co.uk
www.curiousabout.co.uk/brighton
Self-guided walks of discovery, where you can find out more about the place and take part in a treasure hunt.

Helifly

Main Terminal Building, Shoreham Airport, Shoreham By Sea, West Sussex BN43 5FF
www.helifly.co.uk/pdfs/brochure.pdf
Tel: 01273 257070
Try and unique view of Brighton and Hove - from a helicopter. There are also run trips to country houses for lunch or afternoon teas.

i360 Observation Tower

The Brighton i360 observation tower is expected to be completed in 2016. It will be 162 metres (531.49 feet) high! Taller than the London Eye. The observation pod will rise to 138 metres (452.75 feet. www.brightoni360.co.uk

Brighton is the least religious

- According to the 2011 census Brighton is the least religious places in the UK, 42% of the population said they had no religion, compared to the average in the UK which is 25%.
- 2.6% claimed their religion was Jedi Knight, the largest percentage in the country.

Sourced from article: http://en.wikipedia.org/wiki/Brighton

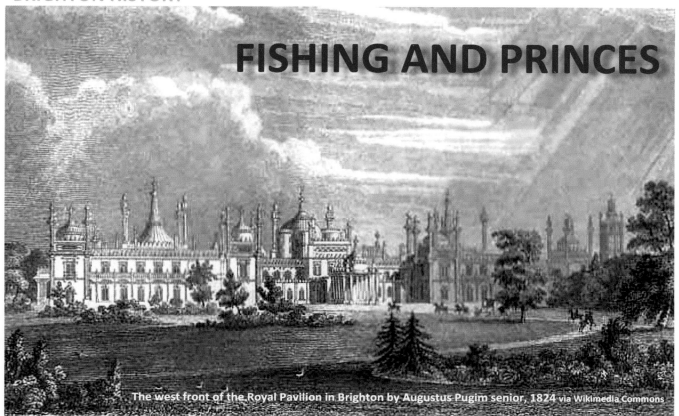

FISHING AND PRINCES

The west front of the Royal Pavilion in Brighton by Augustus Pugim senior, 1824 via Wikimedia Commons

PRINCE REGENT

Above is an illustration of the royal palace of Prince George IV who became Prince Regent in 1811. It was lavishly designed by John Nash in the Indian Indo-Saracenic style. The Prince made it his home as the town had become fashionable for royals and for it's health benefits by the sea.

George's Uncle, Prince Henry, liked gambling, theatre and living life in a flamboyant manner. His nephew shared these passions, and he rented a farmhouse facing the Steine. He soon had it upgraded to the exotic Pavilion. A riding school and stables were built too in the grounds, enough for 60 horses. As it was away from London and the Royal Court, the Prince also used it as a discreet location for his affair with Maria Fitzherbert. She was six years older than him, and a 'commoner'. She was also twice widowed and a Roman Catholic. This meant that he would never be able to officially marry her and keep his royal titles. Yet he still managed to marry her in secret, even though this was not valid, partly because he was already married!

He didn't like his own wife, Caroline of Brunswick and tried to divorce her. George's own father was upright and sturdy. Unlike him, his son led a life of excess, with drinking, mistresses and spending money. George built up debts of what would be the equivalent of 56 million pounds today. By the time he took to the throne at age 57 he was obese and possibly addicted to laudanum. He became ill, spent whole days in bed and suffered from bouts of breathlessness. Since then the Pavilion has not been popular with the royal family and it was sold by the Government to Brighton town in 1850.

FISHING

The mainstay of Brighton for 700 years was fishing. The open land in the town was called the Hempshares. It is the site of the present Lanes. The townsfolk grew hemp for ropes. In Hove, people grew flax to make sails.

The boats were docked in dry land on the Old Steine. The fishermen lived and worked on the beach below the East Cliff. As Brighton grew, many fishermen moved to the Carlton Hill area. Here they would cure and smoke their catches.

The Banqueting Room - John Nash's Views of the Royal Pavilion (1826) via Wikimedia Commons

The Royal Pavilion

The interior is pictured above. It was an opulent palace for lavish parties, dinners and dancing. It is full of Indian and Chinese decorations and design. A huge palm tree in the middle of the ballroom and chandeliers. There is a music room, a banqueting room and saloon. The kitchen is huge and was used to serve magnificent feasts. During World War I it was used as a hospital for Indian soldiers.

Sourced from article: http://en.wikipedia.org/wiki/Royal_Pavilion

The Day Sussex Died - World War I

The Royal Sussex Regiment took part in the Battle of the Boar's Head at Richebourg-l'Avoué. This was on the eve of the Battle of the Somme in 1916. Over 5 hours the 17 officers and 349 men were killed, including 12 sets of brothers, including three from one family. This tragic event became known as the 'Day Sussex Died'.

The Swing Riots

Not anything to do with jazz music or dancing! The Swing Riots were a widespread uprising by farm workers. Threshing machines were taking over manual labour in the 1830s and farm workers were becoming destitute. Eventually the farmers agreed to raise wages. The riots included damaging farm equipment and marches, but also threatening letters, often signed Captain Swing.

Pre-Roman Monuments

WHITEHAWK CAMP - The first settlement in Brighton - around 3000 BC. Neolithic site - four concentric circles of ditches and mounds. Archaeologists found burial mounds, tools and bones

RETAIL PARK OLD SHOREHAM ROAD - The Goldstone - Believed to be a ceremonial stone, which may have formed an ancient circle. In the early 1900s a local farmer was fed up of tourists looking at the stones and had the largest one buried.

HOLLINGBURY CAMP - Celtic Iron Age encampment.

CISSBURY RING - May have been the Celtic tribal capital for the area.

Brighton & Hove through the Ages

3500 BC - Neolithic site on Whitehawk Camp.

1000 BC - British Celts - Hollingbury Camp, Cissbury Ring.

100 AD - The Romans arrive, and built villas in Sussex and Brighton. The villa was built just south of Preston Park, by a stream that used to run down London Road.

500 AD - 'Bristelmestune' - founded by Anglo-Saxon invaders.

1086 - Domesday Book- Fishing for herring and farming village. Population 400.

1400 - Parish church, a market and first constable (in 1285).

1520 - Sacked and burned by French Invaders - Admiral Pregent de Bidoux's. However the town recovered because it had a good mackerel fishing industry. The Old Laines were already established. Population grows quickly.

1580 - Brighton's 80-boat, 10,000-net fleet was the largest in southern England and employed 400 men.

1600 - population 1,500

1640 - population 4000. Brighton is Sussex's most important and biggest town.

1703 - Great Storm

1730 - Town declines, affected by the dwindling fish industry and the growth of Shore ham. Population 2,000. However, drinking and bathing in seawater becomes popular. Dr Richard Russell, from Lewes, sent many patients to 'take the cure' in Brighton sea. The Royal Albion, in Lewes, used to be his house.

1760s - Boarding point for boats travelling to France.

1780s - Georgian terraces started to be built.

1783 - Prince Regent visited Brighton and built the Royal Pavilion by the architect John Nash. It is notable for its Indo-Saracenic architecture and Oriental interior.

1801 - Population 7,000.

1823 - Chain Pier built by Captian Samuel Grown. Lasted until 1896.

1841 - London and Brighton Railway opened.

1864 - Grand Hotel built.

1866 - West Pier built.

1899 - Palace Pier.

1901 - Population 120,000.

1928 - Major expansion of town into Mouselcoomb, Bevendean, Whitehawk, Rottingdean, Patcham, Woodingdean.

1961 - Population 160,000.

1997 - Brighton and Hove joined to form unitary authority of Brighton and Hove and granted city status by Queen Elizabeth II.

Sourced from article: http://en.wikipedia.org/wiki/History_of_Brighton

Chain Pier in Brighton by J. M. W. Turner via Wikimedia Commons

DID YOU KNOW?

CELTS!

Brythonic Celts arrived in Britain 3000 years ago and settled in Hollingbury Hill. These Celts lived in England during the Roman era but after the Anglo Saxons, were pushed into Wales, Cornwall and southern Scotland. Cissbury Ring, 10 miles from Hollingbury may have been the tribal 'capital'.

ROMANS!

The Romans had a large villa at Preston Village, and a Roman road to London was built. After the Romans left Brighton returned to the Celts.

SAXONS!

The Kingdom of Sussex, formed by the Anglo Saxons in 477 AD was ruled by King AElle and his three sons Cymen, Wlencing and Cissa. He battled the Celts and massacred all at Pevensey. The rest are said to have fled to the Forest of Andred.

FORESTS

Sussex used to be covered in forest, the 'Forest of Andred' known today as the Weald, which was 120 miles wide, 30 miles deep. It was so deep that even the Domesday Book didn't record some of the settlements. Wolves, boars and maybe even bears lived there.

CAPITAL

The capital of the Kingdom of Sussex was Chichester, with the Bishop at Selsey. The Kings would have lived at Kingsham. Ditchling would have been an important centre until Lewes. This was because of it's strategic place between the Rivers Adur and Ouse.

POPULATION

450 AD Sussex population 25,000.
1100 AD - 35,000.
1086 (Domesday Book):
Chichester 1200-1500
Lewes 1200
Steyning 600
Pevensey 500
Brighthelmstone 400.

SMUGGLERS & REGENCY IN 'HOVE ACTUALLY'

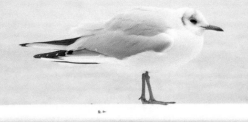

Photo by Davide Ragusa

Hove is an ancient settlement. It grew up alongside Brighton or 'Brighthelmstone' as a very quiet place for many centuries. In the 12th century the parish church, St Andrew's Church was built. It still only had one single street until the 16th century, when even the church was in ruins. The Ship Inn was built around 1702. However in 1801 there were still only 101 residents.

By 1821, the year George IV was on the throne, Hove was still a small village but the population had risen to 312. The houses were mostly around Hove Street, and the rest of the built up areas now were still open farmland.

The isolation was ideal for smuggling. Hove smugglers gained a reputation, and stolen goods from ships were stored in the now partially repaired St. Andrew's Church. The Ship Inn was said to be a favourite meeting place for the smugglers. In 1818 there was a battle on Hove beach between soldiers and smugglers, with the smugglers winning the fight. The Government was determined to crack down on this and a coastguard station was opened at the southern end of Hove Street in 1831, right next to The Ship Inn.

Believe it or not, the bottom of Hove Street was once a bull-ring. In 1810 the bull escaped, scattering spectators before being recaptured. That was the last bull baiting that took place here.

The Brunswick estate of large Regency houses was developed as nearby Brighton became fashionable, and there was a steady rise in population. It's wide roads and grand Regency squares attracted many well known people. Marlborough Court was once the residence of the Duchess of Marlborough, aunt of Winston Churchill. The Irish nationalist leader Charles Stewart Parnell used to visit his lover, Kitty O'Shea in Medina Villas, Hove.

Unconfirmed, but apparently Laurence Olivier (who lived in Brighton, actually) was the origin of the phrase 'Hove, actually'.

Famous Brighton & Hove Residents

Actors & Musicians

Beardyman Moved to Brighton in 2001 to study at the University of Sussex.

Cate Blanchett Lived in Brighton for several years in the mid-2000s.

Dave Gibbons, comic book illustrator, famed for co-creating Watchmen.

David Courtney, born David Cohen in Whitehawk, composer and record producer; discovered and co-wrote with Leo Sayer; also nephew of Henry Cohen who conceived and built Brighton Marina.

David Gilmour, guitarist and vocalist of Pink Floyd, owns house in Hove.

Gaz Coombes, lead singer of band Supergrass, once lived in Brighton.

Neil Megson, performance artist, also known as Genesis P-Orridge.

Nick Cave, Australian musician, writer, and film maker.

Richard Addinsell Composer of the Warsaw Concerto and many film soundtracks. Lived at Chichester Terrace, Kemp Town between 1960 and 1977.

Simon Callow, British actor, has a house in Hove.

Simon Fanshawe, broadcaster, writer, and comedian, lives in Kemptown.

Steve Coogan, comedian well known as Alan Partridge.

Vivien Leigh, actress, Scarlet O'Hara in Gone with the Wind.

Political & Historial Figures

Admiral Sir Edward Codrington, hero of the Battle of Navarino — lived in 140 Western Road (1828–52); a blue commemorative plaque adorns the house

Charles Busby, Regency architect, prolific in Brighton. Lived in Lansdowne Place. House is adorned by a blue commemorative plaque.

Charles Stewart Parnell, Irish politician, died in Brighton.

Edward Booth Went to school in Brighton and lived there until his death in 1890. His collection of specimens is now in the Booth Museum of Natural History.

George Canning, British politician and Prime Minister; resident in 1827

George, Prince of Wales, Prince Regent, and later King George IV of the United Kingdom.

Isambard Kingdom Brunel, engineer, attended Dr Morell's school on Hove seafront, close to Hove Street, for several years from 1820.

John Constable, Romantic painter, intermittently lived in Brighton, calling it "Piccadilly by the Seaside". Resided at 11 Sillwood Road.

Ken Livingstone, politician; formerly Mayor of London; had a house in the Seven Dials area.

Kitty O'Shea, wife of Charles Stewart Parnell.

Maria Fitzherbert, illegitimate wife of George IV (the marriage of a Catholic to a member of the British Royal Family was illegal).

Robert Thomas Flower, 8th Viscount Ashbrook, Irish aristocrat, Lieutenant-Colonel in the British Army, and inventor. Lived at 22 Adelaide Crescent, Hove, in the 1860s.

Sir Winston Churchill, journalist and politician; attended a school run by the "Misses Thompson" in Hove.

William Addison Physician and Fellow of the Royal Society Died in Brighton in 1881

Famous - Miscellaneous

Aleister Crowley, occultist author, died in a nursing home in Hastings, in December 1947; ashes scattered at Devil's Dyke.

Chris Eubank, ex-boxer, who holds the purchased title of "Lord of the Manor of Brighton".

Henry Allingham Supercentenarian and formerly the world's oldest man Moved to St Dunstan's care home at Ovingdean and died there in 2009 aged 113.

Raymond Briggs, artist, writer and illustrator of many children's books including The Snowman, taught at Brighton Art College.

Robin Cousins, figure skater, won gold at 1980 Olympics, lives in Brighton.

Rudyard Kipling, author; lived in Rottingdean between 1897 and 1903.

Steve Ovett, Olympic runner, 800 metres gold medalist in 1980, born and brought up in Brighton. There was a statue of him in Preston Park, Brighton, which got stolen, and a replacement statue is in Madeira Drive. Ovett was made Freeman of the city in July 2012.

Valerie Arkell-Smith Crossdressing woman who impersonated an RAF officer and was known as Colonel Sir Victor Barker. Moved into the Grand Hotel in 1923.

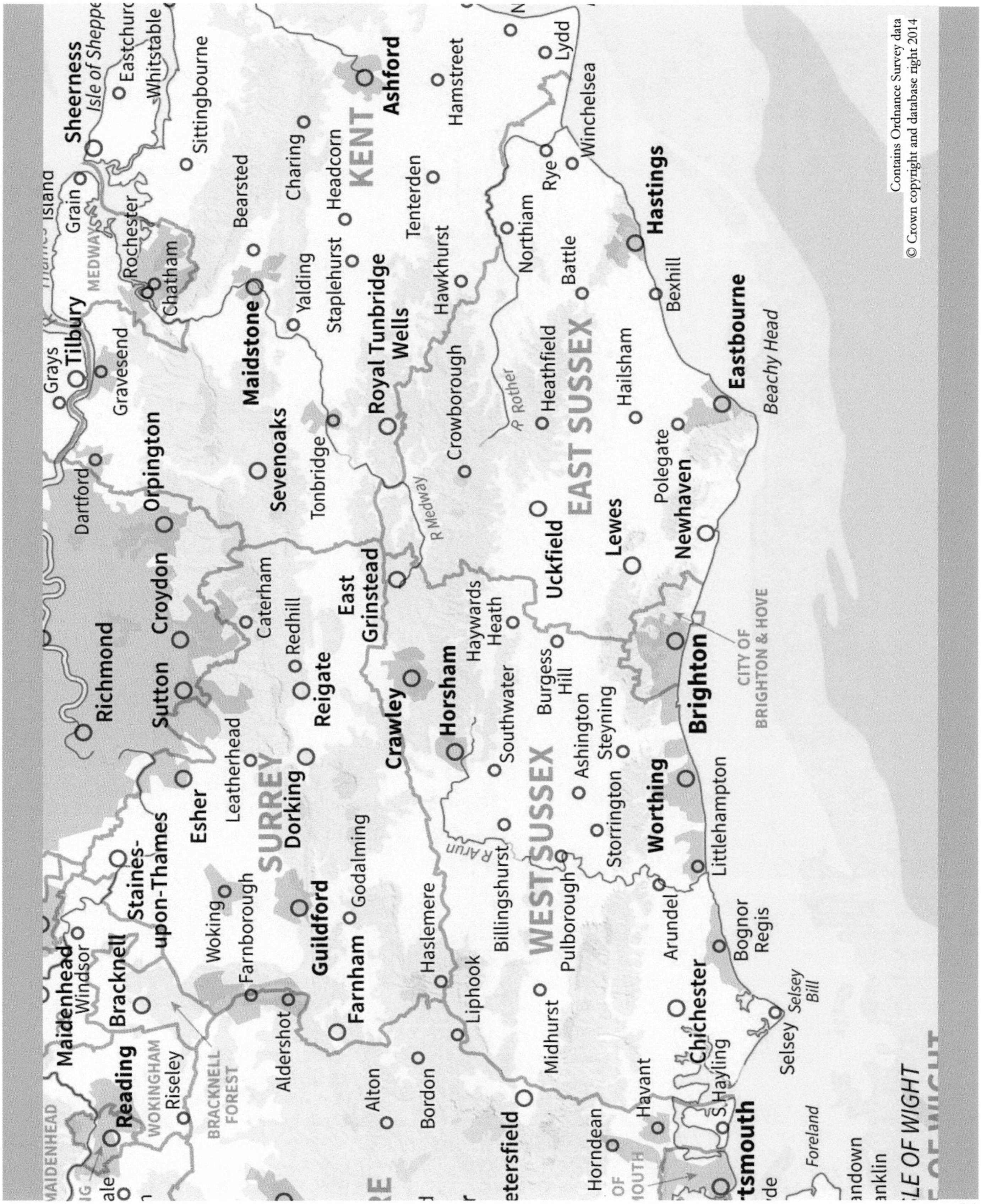
Sheerness
Whitstable
Sittingbourne
Grain
MEDWAY
Rochester
Chatham
Tilbury
Grays
Gravesend
Dartford
Richmond
Sutton
Croydon
Orpington
Maidstone
Bearsted
Charing
Headcorn
KENT
Ashford
Hamstreet
Lydd
Rye
Winchelsea
Tenterden
Hawkhurst
Staplehurst
Yalding
Royal Tunbridge Wells
Sevenoaks
Tonbridge
Crowborough
R Medway
Northiam
Battle
Hastings
Bexhill
R Rother
Heathfield
EAST SUSSEX
Hailsham
Eastbourne
Beachy Head
Polegate
Newhaven
Lewes
Uckfield
Haywards Heath
East Grinstead
Caterham
Redhill
Reigate
Crawley
Horsham
Burgess Hill
Southwater
Brighton
CITY OF BRIGHTON & HOVE
Ashington
Steyning
Storrington
Worthing
Littlehampton
Leatherhead
SURREY
Dorking
Esher
Staines-upon-Thames
Woking
Farnborough
Guildford
Godalming
Haslemere
Billingshurst
WEST SUSSEX
R Arun
Pulborough
Arundel
Bognor Regis
Chichester
Selsey Bill
Selsey
Midhurst
Liphook
Farnham
Aldershot
Bracknell
Windsor
Maidenhead
Reading
WOKINGHAM
Riseley
BRACKNELL FOREST
Alton
Bordon
Havant
S.Hayling
Horndean
Foreland
Contains Ordnance Survey data
© Crown copyright and database right 2014

SUSSEX

Sussex is a beautiful county, with the gentle rolling hills of the South Downs, the stunning white chalk cliffs and seaside towns. There is a huge amount to do with the family. There are relatively easy walks for little feet up to the top of hills that have stunning views over the countryside and sea.

The South Downs have a section to themselves as there is so much to explore, from Birling Gap to pretty little villages, to the mysterious Long Man of Wilmington. At Newhaven Fort there are vast tunnels built into the chalk cliffs. Chanctonbuy and Cissbury Rings are steeps in history and legend.

Or visit a farm where you can feed pigs or have a ride in a tractor, such as Spring Barn Farm. The Sheep Centre at the Seven Sisters has Thomas the Tank Engine as well as over 50 breeds of sheep. Or for the more exotic, visit the Birds of Prey Centres or the Llama Park at Ashdown Forest. Drusillas Park is one of the biggest family attractions in the area

For a look into history, take a journey to Saddlescombe Farm or the Chattri War Memorial to Indian soldiers, which are both very near Brighton.

Castles

Arundel Castle
Arundel, West Sussex BN18 9AB
Tel: 01903 882173 www.arundelcastle.org
Built in the 11th century and set in 40 acres of open ground and lovely formal gardens. It is a magnificent castle. Open year round. The castle was restored in

Bodiam Castle via Wikimedia Commons

1900, and now it's home to the Duke and Duchess of Norfolk and their family. The gardens are redesigned as the garden was neglected during the war. The only flowers in the gardens are catalpas, magnolias and shrubs.

Bodiam Castle
Bodiam, near Robertsbridge, East Sussex, TN32 5UA
www.nationaltrust.org.uk/bodiam-castle
It's history is a bit of mystery, it may have been a defensive castle or built as a home. It is now owned by the National Trust, and opens its doors to the public all year round. The interior was destroyed during the Civil War and only restored relatively recently. The imposing moat is the only surviving water feature. It has a nice tearoom and it can be quite fairytale like for children to visit. It is three miles

off the main A21 at Hurst Green, midway between Hastings and Tunbridge Wells.

Herstmonceux Castle
Hailsham , East Sussex BN27 1RN
Tel: 01323 834444
www.herstmonceux-castle.com
An impressive 15th century castle set in beautiful grounds and parkland. It has woodland trails and a playground. The Castle is on the same site as the Observatory Science Centre. It is set amid beautiful Elizabethan gardens. Woodhenge, the Folly and lake, Rhododendron Gardens and more.
Admission Rates: Adults: £8.00; Children: £5.00

Houses & Gardens

Alfriston Clergy House
The Tye, Alfriston, East Sussex BN26 5TL
Tel: 01323 871961
A 14th Century Wealden Hall House with thatch and timber frame. It was the first house acquired by the National Trust in 1896. It is near the South Downs Way.

Amberley Museum and Heritage Centre
Amberley, nr Arundel
Tel: 01798 831370
www.amberleymuseum.co.uk
36 acres of open-air museum looking at the industrial heritage of the southeast. The museum is also home to a

number of resident craftspeople, who work to traditional methods. There are locomotives, vintage buses, replica buildings and displays. There are also some nature trails and picnic areas.

Borde Hill Garden

Borde Hill Lane, Haywards Heath, West Sussex RH16 1XP
Tel: 01444 450326
info@bordehill.co.uk
www.bordehill.co.uk
This was started in the 1890's. Nd has 200 acres of traditional parkland. There is also a childrens' playground. It is set high in the Sussex High Weald with views across the Ouse Valley Viaduct. It contains an Azalea Ring, for May colour The Italian Garden, centred on a large pool and a Rose Garden planted with 600 David Austin roses and sub-tropical dells.

Bull House

http://sussexpast.co.uk/properties-to-discover/bull-house
Bull House is the headquarters of Sussex Archaeological Society. From 1768 to 1774 it was the home of revolutionary writer Tom Paine. He was the intellectual inspiration behind the American revolution.

Jack & Jill Windmill

Hassocks BN6 9PG
www.jillwindmill.org.uk
Jill is a working corn windmill, built in 1821. Located in the South Downs National Park. If it is a windy day, it can still grind flour. It is not generally open unless the visits are prebooked as groups or through schools, and is more suited for older children. Jack Windmill is in private ownership and is not open to the general public.

High Beeches Garden

High Beeches Ln, Handcross, Haywards Heath, West Sussex RH17 6HQ
www.highbeeches.com
See it in May for the bluebells in it's 27 acres of ancient woodland. This is a landscaped woodland garden that dates from the early 20th century. Ar-

Clayton Windmill via Wikimedia Commons

CLAYTON MILLS NEAR BRIGHTON.

guably the best natural, acid wildflower meadow in Sussex; and a Tree Trail, with 23 trees from different origins.

Merriments Garden

Hawkhurst Road, Hurst Green, East Sussex TN19 7RA
www.merriments.co.uk

Begun in the 1990's, the gardens have matured into a wonderful garden. There is a wild area with birds, butterflies and bees. A bridge leads visitors through the tropical plants and a hot border garden is stunning in the summer.

The National Trust

www.nationaltrust.org.uk
Tel: 0844 8001895

Many historic and beautiful sites are protected by the National Trust. If you like visiting National Trust sites often then you may want to be a member to get discounted rates.

Membership gives access to over 350 gardens, historic houses and castles in the UK. Fees vary but as an example annual membership for an individual paying by direct debit is £43.50, Child £20.25 Family £73.50 (introductory rate). Children under 5 go free. (2014 prices).

Marlipins Museum

39 High Street, Shoreham-by-Sea, West Sussex, BN43 5DA
Tel: 01273 462994
http://sussexpast.co.uk/properties-to-discover/marlipins-museum
A distinctive building, 12th to 13th Century with a chess board flint and Caen limestone facade. It is one of the oldest buildings in Sussex. No one knows exactly what it's original use, perhaps it was a storehouse, or a hospital.

Deeds survive from 1347, when it was an Oat Market. Currently it houses archaeology and the story of the area, including the Shoreham Beach film industry, which was once the centre of the silent movie hub of England.
Open: from 10.30 am to 4.30 pm, Tuesday to Saturday, May to October.
Admission: Adult: £2.50 Child: £1

Nymans Gardens

Handcross, near Haywards Heath, West Sussex, RH17 6EB
Tel: 01444 405250
www.nationaltrust.org.uk/nymans
A National Trust garden set in the High Weald. It is a beautiful place, with ancient woods and rare flowers. Built in the late 1800's by Ludwig Messel. He created a garden with plants collected from around the world. The romantic ruins of a fairy-tale gothic mansion remain. For children there are natural play trails, geocaching in the garden and woods, pick up and go activities and school holiday trails.

Petworth House & Gardens

Petworth, West Sussex, GU28 0AE
Tel: 01798 342207
petworth@nationaltrust.org.uk
www.nationaltrust.org.uk/petworth house
Majestic 17th-century country house in a 700-acre deer park, landscaped by 'Capability' Brown and painted by Turner. The interior has artworks from Turner and others, including Van Dyck, Reynolds and Blake, ancient and Neo-classical sculpture.

Sheffield Park

Uckfield, East Sussex, TN22 3QX
Tel 01825 790231
sheffieldpark@nationaltrust.org.uk
www.nationaltrust.org.uk/sheffield park-and-garden
Four lakes are central to the garden design. Paths wind through the glades and wooded areas. There is a Palm Walk and lovely gardens.

The Sheffield Park estate has had many uses, including a deer park and WWII camp. Now it has a natural woodland play trail in Ringwood Toll. The River Ouse runs across the bottom of the parkland.

Southover Grange & Gardens

Southover Road, Lewes, East Sussex BN7 1AB
www.lewes.gov.uk/business/11757.asp
Built in the 16th Century, it is a pretty house now used as a school and venue. It houses a craft shop and cafe. The gardens a lovely, with a knot garden, Magnolias, a mulberry tree hundreds of years old, a tulip tree, wildflower area and stream. In summer there are many families and people here having picnics or at the tea rooms.

Sussex Prairies Garden

Morlands Farm, Wheatsheaf Road, Henfield BN5 9AT

Sheffield Park via Wikimedia Commons

Tel: 01273 495902
www.sussexprairies.co.uk
A bit of a hidden gem, and surprisingly fun with kids. It is only open in summer to autumn. There are tall prairie plants swishing about in the wind, a glass sculpture and a lovely cakes. You can get a great bunch of country flowers for £5 too.

The Priest House

North Lane, West Hoathly, West Sussex, RH19 4PP.
Tel: 01342 810479
http://sussexpast.co.uk/properties-to-discover/the-priest-house
A historic 15th Century house owned by Henry VIII, Thomas Cromwell, Anne of Cleves, Mary I and Elizabeth I. It is now furnished with 17th & 18th century country furniture
Open: March to October 10.30am to 5.30pm. Sunday 12pm opening. Closed Mondays except Bank Holidays.
Admission: Adult £4.00, child £2.00, concessions £3.50, family £10.00 (1 adult and 4 children, or 2 adults and 2 children), Garden only £1.00.

Wakehurst Place

Ardingly, Haywards Heath, West Sussex, RH17 6TN
Tel: 01444 894066
wakehurst@kew.org
www.nationaltrust.org.uk/wakehurst-place
This is a botanical garden with the world's largest seed conservation project. It is the country estate of the Royal Botanic Gardens, Kew. It has science-based plant conservation and research. There are natural woodland and lakes, formal gardens and an Elizabethan house.

Scenic & Fun Railways

Bluebell Railway

Sheffield Park Station, East Sussex TN22 3QL
info@bluebell-railway.co.uk
Tel: 01825 720800

Old 'Daddy Long Legs' Railway Poster. Also shows Volks Electric Railway
Photo via Wikimedia Commons

www.bluebell-railway.com
Steam trains between Sheffield Park and East Grinstead. There are popular special events such as the Santa and Fairy Godmother specials.

Hove Park Miniature Railway

www.hoveparkrailway.co.uk
Open from March to October, fares are a reasonable £1 for adults, 50 for children. It is open usually once a month, more in the summer, check the website for details.

Kent & East Sussex Railway Company

Tenterden Town Station, Station Road, Tenterden, Kent TN30 6HE
www.kesr.org.uk
A rural light railway winding from Tenterden for ten miles through the countryside of the Rother Valley to the magnificent National Trust castle at Bodiam.

Lavender Line

Isfield Station, Near Uckfield, East Sussex TN22 5XB

Tel: 08457 484950
www.lavender-line.co.uk
The railway travels between the village of Isfield and Worth hal, a round trip of 2 miles. It is called the Lavender Line after a local coalmerchant A.E Lavender who had his coal merchant office located by the cattle dock at Isfield station.

Miniature Steam Railway Adventure Park

Lottbridge Drove, Eastbourne, East Sussex BN23 6QJ.
Tel: 01323 520229
www.emsr.co.uk
A miniature steam railway set in a country park. It goes around a five acre lake and has lovely tea rooms. These are one-eighth scale miniature locomotives There are also prize winning tea rooms.

Volks Railway

Brighton Seafront, east of the Pier to the Marina
Britain's oldest electric railway built in 1883, running for one and a quarter miles.

History and Science

Bignor Roman Villa

Bignor Roman Villa, Bignor, West Sussex RH20 1PH
Tel: 01798 869259
It is situated high in the Downs, near footpaths which lead onto the countryside in many directions. You can see how the Roman designers signed their work with a dolphin. It also has a working farm.

Fishbourne Roman Palace & Gardens

Fishbourne Roman Palace, Roman Way, Fishbourne, West Sussex, PO19 3QR
Tel: 01243 785859
http://sussexpast.co.uk/properties-to-discover/fishbourne-roman-palace
Only discovered in 1960, this is the largest Roman home in Britain. It was built 2000 years ago, after the Roman

Fishbourne Palace via Wikimedia Commons

conquest of Britain. A rectangular Roman Palace, still with many beautiful mosaics including an intact dolphin mosaic. It had underfloor heating, a bath house and has a larger footprint than Buckingham Palace! The gardens have been replanted in the original Roman period, so you can imagine what it may have been like to be of Roman nobility, wandering the grounds.

2014 Opening times

January open Saturdays & Sundays only: 10am – 4pm

February open every day: 10am – 4pm

March - October open every day: 10am – 5pm

November – 15 Dec open every day: 10am – 4pm

From 16th -31st December open Saturdays and Sundays only: 10am – 4pm

2014 Admission: Adult £8.70, child £4.30, concessions £7.70, family (2+2 or 1+4) £22.00. Admission price for groups of 15+: Adults/students/seniors £7.00, children £3.50.

We wunt be druv

This is the Sussex motto. It means 'we will not be pushed around'.

The name "Sussex" is derived from the Middle English Suthsæxe, meaning land or people.

Foredown Tower Countryside Centre

Foredown Road, Portslade, BN41 2EW

Tel: 01273 292092

foredown.tower@brighton-hove.gov.uk

As well as providing great views across the downs this early 20th century Edwardian tower is appealing to those interested in science, nature and the environment. It has exhibitions and is home to an operational camera obscura.

Newhaven Fort

Fort Road, Newhaven, East Sussex BN9 9DS

Tel: 01273 517622

www.newhavenfort.org.uk

A good example of an English fortification. The Fort has some great exhibits that conjure up the sights, sounds and even smells of the period. Explore the huge, eery tunnels built into the chalk cliffs. It is a 10-acre site with great views of the South Downs and Sussex Coast.

Newhaven Fort is open from March to October.

What is the highest point in Sussex?

Blackdown is the highest point in Sussex at 280metres.

Ditchling Beacon is the second highest point at 248 metres.

Tickets: Adult £6.00 per ticket; Child (4-15) £4.00 per ticket

Observatory Science Centre

Herstmonceux, Hailsham, East Sussex, BN27 1RN

Tel: 01323 832731

The Observatory Science Centre is set in the middle of the countryside in Herstmonceux, away from light pollution. It is in the same parkland as the Castle.

The South Downs Planetarium

Kingsham Farm, Kingsham Road, Chichester, PO19 8RP

Tel: 01243 774400

www.southdowns.org.uk

Both educational and entertaining the planetarium can offer you sights that you may not see for real. This artificial sky enables you to view a comet much like the real thing, or a meteor, an eclipse of the moon.

Paradise Park

Avis Road, Newhaven BN9 0DH

Tel: 01273 512123

www.paradisepark.co.uk

It has a Museum of Life for fossils, crystals and minerals. Planet Earth displays the story of the world. Sure to be a favourite is the park with life size model dinosaurs. There is an adventure play area and fun trail, plus a crazy golf course.

Boat Trips

Sussex Voyages

Lower Quayside, The Waterfront, Sovereign Marina, Eastbourne, East Sussex BN25 6JH

Tel: 01293 888780

www.sussexvoyages.co.uk

See the Sussex coast by boat, from Beachy Head and the Royal Sovereign Light Tower.

Tickets: Adult from £18.00 to £25.00 Child (4-16 years) from £14.00 to £18.00 per ticket; Infant (3 years old & under) £5.00 per ticket

Boat Trip

Brighton, BN2 5UP
www.brightonmarina.co.uk
Take a pleasure boat trip from Brighton Marina and see Brighton from a different perspective.

Ross Boat Trips

Pontoon 5, West Jetty, Brighton Marina Village, Brighton BN2 5UP
Tel: 07958 246414
Bookings for individuals and groups of up to 60 people per boat. Pleasure trips, power boat rides, mackerel fishing trips.
90 minute mackerel fishing trip - £20 per person - Spectators £10 per person
45 minute pleasure trips - £7.50 per Adult - £5 per child under 12 years
25 minute power boat rides - £15 per person

Theme & Activity Parks

Harbour Park

Seafront, Littlehampton, West Sussex
BN17 5LH
Tel: 01903 721200
www.harbourpark.com
This is located near the beach and has children's rides including Logger's Revenge Water Chute and Caterpillar Coaster. Free Entry.

Go Ape

Go Ape Crawley - Tilgate Park, Crawley, West Sussex
RH10 5PQ
Go Ape Bedgebury - Bedgebury Road, Goudhurst, Cranbrook, Kent
TN17 2SJ
http://goape.co.uk
Award-winning outdoor activities, including swinging and zip wiring through the trees. The over 10's can take part in the classic Tree Top Adventure. Anyone over 1 metre can get off the ground and up in the trees with Tree Top Junior.

Sunniest place in the UK!

The coast of Sussex and Hampshire are the sunniest places in the UK. The sea breezes blow away the clouds. The hot humid weather in summer and cold spells in winter are due to the closeness to the continent of Europe.

Where is the Tornado Hotspot?

Selsey is known as a tornado hotspot. Small tornados have hit the place in 1986, 1998 and 2000. The 1998 tornado damaged 1,000 buildings.

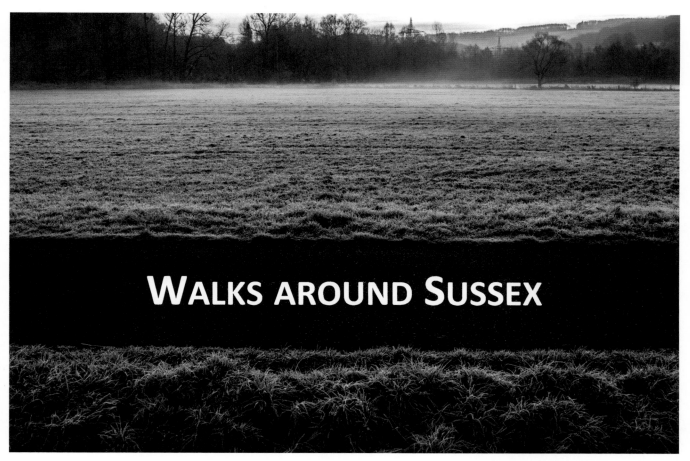

WALKS AROUND SUSSEX

Brighton, Hove and the South Downs have a variety of walks that suit children. A stroll along the promenade on the seafront is always refreshing. It has the added bonus of being near cafes, museums and the Pier. There are some great local parks, such as Queen's Park and Preston Park.

You don't have to go far to feel out in the countryside. The green rolling hills of the South Downs are beautiful. They may lack the majesty of mountains but they more than make up for it with a tranquil serenity. And because they are more gentle, they can be less tiring for little legs.

From the valley of Cuckmere Haven, to the pretty village of King-ston near Lewes. Enjoy the breathtaking views at Hollingbury Fort or Chanctonbury Ring. Explore ancient forests with beeches, birches and yew trees hundreds of years old in Stanmer Park. Amble through the purple blue blanket of bluebells in Arlington forest.

To make walks more interesting, children of all ages can be inspired by a bit of knowledge about an areas social and geological history. For example did you know there Sussex was an important area for the British Celtic people? Or that Chanctonbury Ring was used by the Roman's as a religious site?

Walk to see nature like the autumn leaves, birds, insects or even bats. The South Downs is a unique hab-itat for wildlife. There are some rare butterflies and birds such as the skylark. Walking can be a great way for kids to discover and wonder nature. From the crickets in the summer to the scampering of squirrels in the autumn.

Or make mini detective out of your kids, with treasure walks or 'geocaching'. Whatever the weather, it's great to get outdoors.

Photo by Andre Koch

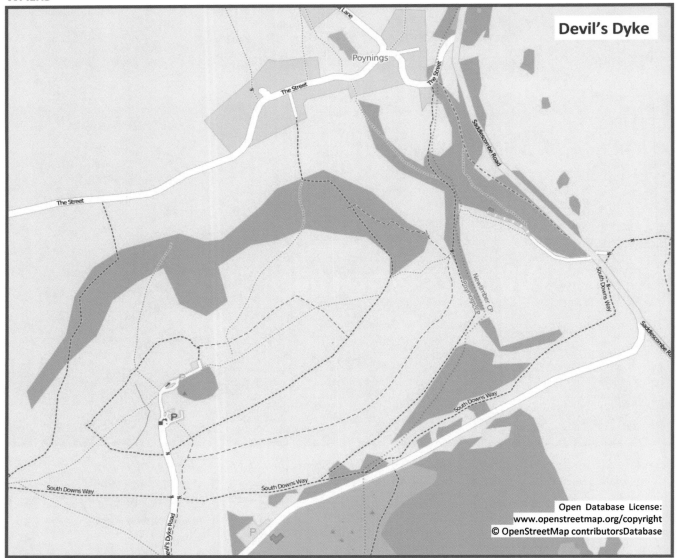

Devil's Dyke

Short Local Walks

Devil's Dyke Walk

There are some steep and narrow parts to this walk, so may not be suitable for all ages.

1. Start at Devil's Dyke car park at the pub. Go back towards the Devil's Dyke pub sign, follow the path alongside the road until you get to a gate on your left.

2. Head down the valley then make turn sharply right after 50 yards and go through a gate into a deep valley.

On the right of the valley is the concrete footings of the great cableway.

3. There should be two humps ahead which are the Devil's graves.

4. Go through a small gate at the right, go up the path and turn sharply right up a steep footpath which leads to a stile. Go along the field with telegraph poles in it, and head up the tarmac track and through the gate at the top.

5. Cross the road and go into Saddlescombe Farm, past the pond

on your right. The Hiker's Rest tearoom is after a barn on the left. There is a donkey wheel here.

6. To start your journey back, retrace your steps out of the farm and down the road. Turn left sharply, past the trough and then right above te fence and ditch. Go straight over the field and at the top go over a stile. Turn right down a very steep bank. If it's too steep you can continue on the path down and zig zag your way down.

7. Take the stile are the left o the fence and climb the steps up to the woods.

40

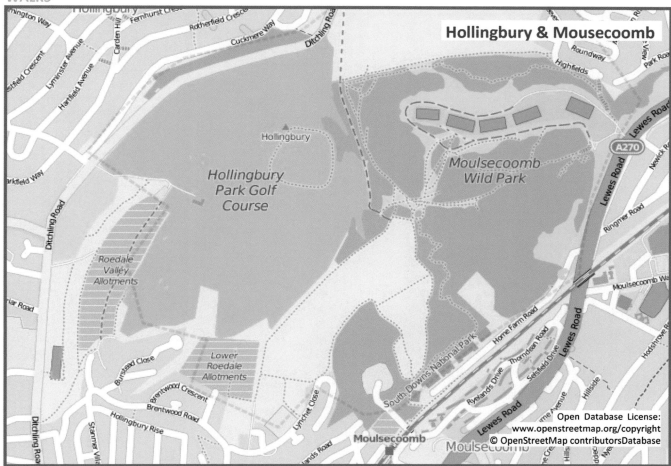

Hollingbury & Mousecoomb

Follow the six steps across the path at the crossroads.

8. At the kissing gate, go up a steep 63 steps to see the stunning view. It is very steep so you will need to take care. Continue up the narrow path until you get to another kissing gate. Head back to the pub.

Hollingbury

Distance: 2 miles
Grading: Easy/moderate

1. Start at Ditchling Road, and head to Osbourne Road.
2. Turn left onto Hollingbury Park Avenue.
3. Turn left to Hollingbury Rise, and left again to Stanmer Villas.
4. Turn right onto Brentwood Road, then left onto Lynchet Close.

5. Then turn left onto the path that leads up to Hollingbury Gold Course.
6. Skirt around the golf course, with the grounds on your left.
7. You will have the option of going up back onto Ditchling Road, or around back into Mouslecomb or Wild Park to loop back or take the train back from Mouslecomb.

Hove Park

Parkview Road, Hove BN3 7BF
www.brighton-hove.gov.uk/content/leisure-and-libraries/parks-and-green-spaces/hove park

A big park with plenty of space to run around, let off steam or walk with a buggy. 40 acres or grass, trees, flowers and sports facilities. It also has a playground, toilets and cafe. Oh and a miniature steam railway! It has a Fingermaze, football pitches, tennis &

basketball courts and bowling greens. This is a large and pretty park. It has a lovely café. This has sports pitches and facilities, an adventure play

Stanmer Park

This is a lovely 3 mile countryside walk above the rolling hills around Stanmer village. You can stop off at the village for a cup of tea. It is mostly flat with some gentle hills. Take the bus 25 or 78 or it is a short walk from Falmer train station.

1. Start at the entrance to Stanmer, this is where the bus drops you off. Head towards the village, pst the nature reserve and car park to your left.
2. You will pass by the museum as the road forks left, take this road and go past Stanmer House until you get to the church and tea

41

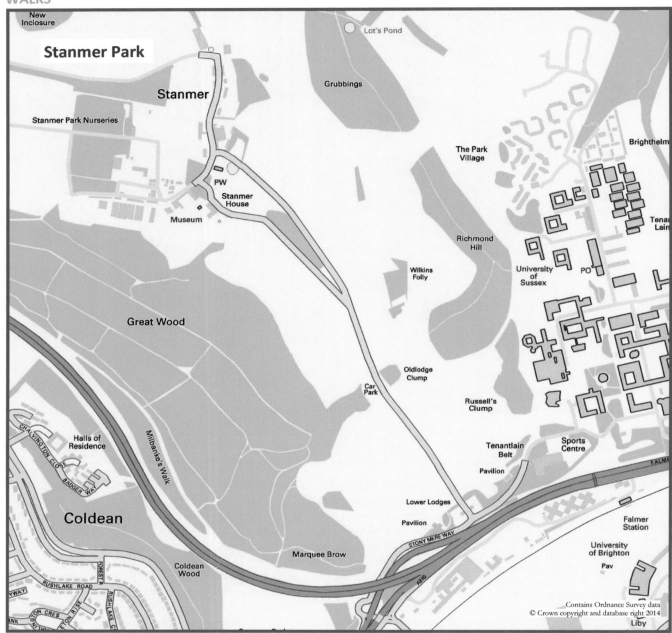

room. Notice the old yew trees in the churchyard.

3. You may want to stop off for a bite to eat. Carry on through Stanmer village until the road turns left. Instead of turning left to the nurseries, head straight on into the countryside.

4. You will pass Limekiln wood to your left, and Bushy Clump to your right. Take the right fork in the path at Limekiln wood.

5. The road bends to the right. Carry on until another T junction, take a sharp right into Millbank Wood.

6. Carry on for about a mile, past the small pond to your left. You can see the University campus to your left on Richmond Hill.

7. Take the right fork by the University down the hill, then it will turn left bringing you back to the entrance of Stanmer Park.

May Bluebell Walks

Arlington Bluebell Walk

Bates Green Farm, Hailsham BN26 6SH, England
Tel: 01323 485151
www.bluebellwalk.co.uk
From mid April to mid May
It will be their 43rd year in 2015. Relatively easy access paths though not all of them wheelchair or buggy friendly, giving a great view of the bluebells.

Over a 40 year period the Arlington Bluebell Walk has raised over £215,000 for 60 local charities

Treasure Hunting

Geocaching
www.geocaching.com
This is a modern day treasure hunt, using a GPS device to find hidden containers or 'caches'. It is a nice, simple idea set up by volunteers worldwide. And it's free. You can put in your postcode and search for nearby caches. You can also find out how to hide your own cache using the guidelines online. They will contain a log book to sign, and a small number of items of low monetary value that you can trade e.g. Key rings, small toys.

Healthwalks
www.brighton-hove.gov.uk/content/leisure-and-libraries/sports-and-activity/healthwalks

This is a City Council initiative, with 18 regular walks across the city. They are from a mile to three miles, so fairly easy and led by trained Volunteer Walk Leaders.

Walks with a Buggy

There are some great walks that you can take with a buggy or a wheelchair. The South Downs official website lists a few, however there are also more such as the under cliff walks and around the towns and along river paths.
www.southdowns.gov.uk/enjoying/outdoor-activities

Devil's Dyke – 1.5 miles
This is near the old railway route that ran from 1887 to 1938. Start at Boundary Halt car park off the A27.

1. Walk from the car park towards Devil's Dyke, with woods on the right and the road to your left.
2. After about half a mile, turn left to go over the road onto the valley floor, slightly downhill for another half a mile.
3. At the path, turn left to go back to the car park.

Dyke Railway Trail – 1.5 miles
This follows the railway route, and you can get the Bus 5b, 16 or 66 from central Brighton.
Start at the Devil's Dyke Trail car park off the A27, first left after the Portslade turning, just before the Downsman pub.

1. A very straightforward walk, follow the Railway trail to the north, crossing over the A27 Lewes/Worthing road.

2. See the Benfield Hill Local Nature Reserve to the west, which has rare wildlife in it's chalky grassland. There is a viewpoint midway, and at the end just after the gate. Turn back after two thirds of a mile.

Beachy Head Peace Path

Less than half a mile. This has wonderful views over the Downs as far as Eastbourne and Hastings, and the sea. Get Bus 33 in the summer from Eastbourne.

1. Start opposite the car park Visitor Centre at Beachy Head.
2. Head over the road towards the sea and the viewpoint, crossing over the grassy path.
3. Turn back, over the ramp, alongside the grassy path, then turn right back to the car park.

Cuckmere Valley

Less than half a mile.
Bus 13 runs via Beachy Head. As you are on the A27 towards Seaford, go through Alfriston and the car park is on the left about a mile before Seaford. There are no toilets or refreshments here.

1. The trail starts above the Litlington White Horse.
2. Start at the car park, and go over the two ramps towards the viewpoints.
3. You can see across the valley to the sea. Then go back the way you came.

Hollingbury Woods

1.5 miles. This is a lovely little walk, taking about an hour. The beech woods were planted about 200 years ago, and the trail is crushed sandstone.

1. Start at Hollingbury Golf Club entrance by the car park, opposite Woodbourne Avenue, off the Hollingbury/Ditchling exit from the A27. There are no toilets or refreshments.
2. Walk down into the woods towards the golf club, but then turn right into the woods. Keep on the main

path past the playground and bowling green on your right.
3. Circle back to the left, into the woods past the Allotments on your right, through the woodland glad and circle left back to the start.

The Undercliff Walk

It starts at Brighton Marina and you can take the Volks Railway here. This can be windy, but so refreshing to walk by the salty crashing waves. It is accessible all the way to Saltdean. There is a great little beach side cafe half way along. Although hang on to your tea on a windy day! There are tea shops in Rottingdean too.

Nature Walks

The South Downs is a special area, nurturing many birds, insects, flowers and animals. In May the woods are a haze of purple blue, carpeted with bluebells.

Some of these are easier to spot than others. There are plenty of wildlowers, grassy mounds, rabbits and birds. In the summer you can hear the crickets. However, if you are lucky you might see roe deer or a hare, or catch a glimpse of the

distinctive red kite flying above. The otter, skylark, brown trout and barn owl also live in this area. Flowers include the burnt orchid, round-headed rampion

You may not have heard of the chalk carpet moth or sundew, a carnivorous plant. Rare species such as the Adonis blue butterfly and silver-spotted skipper butterfly have started to increase thanks to conservation work. is a good example of this. Others, like the nightjar are threatened as they have very particular places they like to live - heathland and open woodland with clearings.

For £3.80 you can get a handy fold-out chart that can help identify common birds, livestock, moths and butterflies and farm crops. It is from the field studies council: www.field-studies-council.org/publications/pubs/features-of-the-south-downs-way.aspx

Bats

As you look at the sky in the evening, you might be lucky enough to spot a bat. The bat flies over the water to feed on insects. Bats are the world's

only flying mammal. They emit their own sonar used to find their prey. They need to eat 3000 insects a night just to stay alive and are very important for our ecosystem. There are bats, the barbastelle bat on the South Downs. The greater mouse-eared bat has only ever been seen in the Downs and has hardly been seen since.

Nature Reserves

Stoneywish Nature Reserve
Spatham Lane, Ditchling BN6 8XH
01273 843498
www.stoneywish.co.uk
A friendly family run 50 acres of wetlands, meadows and woodland, home to wildlife as well as farm animals. Large play area and open space to have a picnic. Children's nature corner, shop and visitor centre.

Bedelands Farm Nature Reserve
Burgess Hill , West Sussex RH15 8AW
Tel: 01444 477561
www.midsussex.gov.uk/7830.htm?pageI
D=2647
This is near Burgess Hill, and there are lovely walks past ponds, woodlands and wild flower meadows. You can get there by a footpath off Valebridge Close and from beneath the viaduct in Valebridge Road. Open late spring to early winter. 9am to 5pm.

Countryside Code

1. Be safe, plan ahead and follow any signs.
2. Leave gates and property as you find them.
3. Protect plants and animals and take your litter home.
4. Keep dogs under close control, and on a lead, especially near farm animals and during nesting season.
5. Consider other people.

British Butterflies
Left
1. Swallow-tail.
2. Brimstone.
3. Clouded Yellow, 3 *a*, female.
4. Pale Clouded Yellow.

Plate III. from W. S. Coleman's British Butterflies (1860).

III.

British Butterflies
Right:
1. Large Blue.
2. Chalk-hill Blue, 2 *a*, female.
3. Adonis Blue, 3 *a*, female.
4. Common Blue, 4 *a*, female.
5. Silver-studded Blue, 5 *a*, female.
6. Brown Argus.
7. Artaxerxes Butterfly. (modern: Northern Brown Argus)

Plate XIV. from W. S. Coleman's British Butterflies (1860).

XIV.

46

THE SOUTH DOWNS

Photo by David Marcu

The South Downs
www.southdowns.gov.uk
"Out blunt, bow-headed whale backed Downs". Rudyard Kipling (lived in Rottingdean).

These are softly rolling green hills and are a beautiful part of Sussex. The white chalk is exposed at cliffs at the Seven Sisters. There are many walking paths and places of special interest. You can't really beat the feeling of a light wind and views down to the sea walking along the top of the hills on a fair day.

It is 670km² or 260 square miles from Hampshire to Beachy Head, near Eastbourne. The South Downs National Park is a larger

area still, including parts of the Weald. The power of the sea's crashing waves create unusual chalk platforms and large chunks of white chalk as the cliffs erode at up to one metre a year.

Places of interest include: Chanctonbury Ring; Seaford Head; Seven Sisters; the Long Man; Clayton Windmills and Beachy Head. Beachy Head is the highest chalk sea cliff in Britain, 531 feet above sea level. Four river valleys cut through: Arun; Adur; Ouse and Cuckmere. You can find little 'dew ponds' around, artificial ponds for cows and sheep.

Sheep and rabbits have grazed the turf over the years to a springy turf - old chalk grassland. Farmers used to alternate sheep grazing with

corn, but after World War II more land was needed for arable farming, and little of this grassland remains (from 40-50% to 3-4%).

Legends and Pagan Rites
Sussex was cut off from most of Engaland by the Weald and was probably the last place to accept Christianity. So Pagan traditions and folklore have a long history in the Downs.

Birling Gap, Beachy Head, Cuckmere Haven & the Seven Sisters

Birling Gap
East Dean, near Eastbourne, East Sussex, BN20 0AB
Tel 01323 423197
www.nationaltrust.org.uk/birling-gap-and-the-seven-sisters

www.sevensisters.org.uk

It is a good starting point for some exhilarating clifftop walks and the Seven Sisters chalk cliffs. The beach, accessible down some steps, is great for rockpools and seaside picnics. It also has one of the most magnificent backdrops in England. There's a pub and café at the top, you can buy fishing nets and buckets and spades here. Birling Gap and Crowlink, near Eastbourne in East Sussex. There are over 500 acres of open chalk grassland the area is rich with butterflies and wild flowers. The Belle Tout neolithic enclosure can be found further along the coast. The Belle Tout lighthouse was moved back from the cliff edge on rollers a few years ago! It just shows how quickly erosion by the sea happens.

Seven Sisters Country Park Visitor Centre

Exceat, Seaford, East Sussex BN25 4AD
Tel: 01323 870280.

The Seven Sisters Country Park comprises 280 hectares of chalk cliffs, meandering river valley and open chalk grassland. You can hire cycles from the Cuckmere Cycle Hire next door, however the woods are too bumpy to take child seats. There have been shipwrecks and you can see pill boxes or guard posts from World War II. There is an 'easy access trail' across the park which is suitable for push chairs and wheelchairs. The trail follows the valley down to the shingle beach and is about 3 miles return.

Getting there: Bus 12, 13, 712 run from Brighton and Eastbourne. Nearest train is Seaford.

Beachy Head & Countryside Centre

www.english-heritage.org.uk/discover/south downs/explore/beachy-head

One of the highest points of the cliffs. This dramatic place is windy and wild. The chalk cliffs are a sheer drop to the

Stanmer Park

Lewes Rd, Brighton, Sussex BN1 9SE
www.brighton-hove.gov.uk/content/leisure-and-libraries/parks-and-green-spaces/stanmer-park

This is a very accessible place from Brighton or Lewes, but very quiet and pretty. There are woodland walks, lovely tea shop, ancient Yew trees and views of the Downs. It is right next to Sussex University you can get off the train here and walk around. Or nearer is the Bus 25 or 78.

Stanmer Tea Rooms
Open: 9.30am - 4pm daily
Stanmer Village is an 18th century working village, with Stanmer House as the main property. Stanmer hosts the annual Sussex Festival of Nature - www.brighton-hove.gov.uk/sfon

Stanmer outdoor activity trails

Beginner trails for walking and Nordic walking followed by trails for cross-country running and off-road family cycling through the Stanmer Experience Project.

crashing waves below. You see the iconic red and white striped lighthouse, in operation since 1902. Discover the history of the downs in the Downland Experience in the Countryside Centre. The Sussex Gallery shows the work of local artists. Countryside Centre open daily from April to October, weekends only November, December and March weather permitting - call 01323 737273 to check, closed January & February.

Cuckmere Valley

East Sussex, BN26 5TT
cuckmere@nationaltrust.org.uk
Tel: 01323 423197
www.nationaltrust.org.uk/cuckmere-valley

This is a lovely place, with a flower-rich chalk grassland and views of views of the Cuckmere River and the Seven Sisters. It can get quite windy near the beach. Cradle Valley is rich in wildlife and colourful butterflies in summer. In 1836 a white horse was cut into the chalk on the steep scarp. Chyngton Farm was ploughed for food during World War II and artefacts, like anti-tank traps, pill boxes

and bunkers, are still there. High and Over's dramatic river cliff has been carved out of the soft chalk by the river below. In 1836 a white horse was cut into the chalk on the steep scarp and it remains a popular natural attraction.

Chyngton Farm was ploughed for food during World War II and artefacts, like anti-tank traps, pill boxes and bunkers, are still visible today.

Historic Hill Forts

Chanctonbury Ring

www.english-heritage.org.uk/discover/south-downs/explore/chanctonbury-cissbury

A hill fort topped with trees, about 794 ft above sea level. It is probably built in the early Iron Age, then abandoned and used by the Romans as a religious site. Two temples stood there, one in classical form, one perhaps a polygon of 11 sides. The beech trees at the top were planted by Charles Goring in 1760. They were

South Downs Bus Walks

www.brighton-hove.gov.uk/content/parking-and-travel/travel-transport-and-road-safety/breeze-downs-0
A series of six leaflets offering 18 easy-to-follow walks on the South Downs. Alternatively they can be sent if you contact local.transport@brighton-hove.gov.uk

Bus Trip to Devil's Dyke

Tel: 01273 292480
www.brighton-hove.gov.uk/breezebuses
The no. 77 bus can be boarded at Brighton Pier as well as other places throughout the city.

Bus Discovery Tickets

Offer one day's unlimited bus travel in Sussex, Surrey and East Hampshire. Issued and accepted by all bus companies: just buy on board the first bus you catch. Family (5 people, max 2 adults) £16, Adult £8.50, Child £7.

77 to Devil's Dyke: £2.90 single, £4.50 Return
78 to Stanmer Park: £2.40 single and £4.50 Return
79 to Ditchling Beacon: £2.90 single, £4.50 Return
Return tickets can be used to return from Devil's Dyke, Stanmer Park or Ditchling Beacon.
Up to two children per adult travel free.
Advanced booking is recommended by telephoning the booking office: 01293 888780

Photo by Martin Dorsch

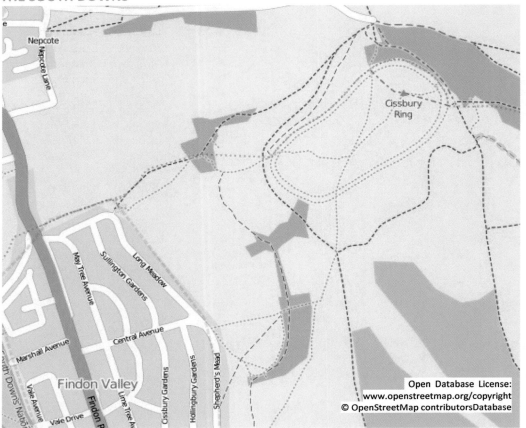

It was used militarily as recently as World War II by the 2nd Argyll and Sutherland Highlanders in preparation for the Normandy Landings. A gap was made in the ramparts for a 45kg gun used to fire at ships in the English Channel. It is well known for ghostly sightings.

Ditchling Beacon

near Ditchling, East Sussex
Tel: 01323 423197
www.nationaltrust.org.uk/ditchling-beacon
This was once the site for a warning beacon. If there were signs of an invasion it would be lit up. It also has the remains of an iron age hill fort. It is worth the walk up here to see the views across the city, to the sea and over the hills. It is about 7 miles to the north of Brighton and just south of the village of Ditchling.

Please note: Payment for parking is the RingGo system – either use the RingGo smartphone apps on the site or call ahead from home on 01372 885500. All you need to start is your car's registration and the Ditchling Beacon location number 8507. You will also be asked to key in your credit or debit card number.

Shoreham Fort

www.shorehamfort.co.uk
It is also known as Kingston or Shoreham Redoubt and was built 1857 in case of French attack. The Fort is a de-

thickly wooded until the Great Storm of 1987, which destroyed many.

The legend locally is that the Ring was created by the Devil and that he can be summoned by running around the trees 7 times anti-clockwise. He will appear and offer a bowl of soup in exchange for your soul!

Cissbury Ring

Near Findon, West Sussex, BN14 0HT
www.nationaltrust.org.uk/cissbury-ring
The largest hill fort in Sussex and second largest in England, covering 60 acres. It was built probably around 250 years BC but abandoned 200 years or so later. There are ancient flint mines around, excavated with antler picks. Flint was used for stone axes.

There is a great view from the top, you can even see to the Isle of Wight on a clear day, and to Chichester Cathedral. For kids it is great to fly a kite up here. During spring and autumn you can see many migratory birds as Cissbury is one of the first landing points after their long flight across the sea.

Did you know that Chalk is made of creatures?!

Chalk is made up of coccoliths from coccolithophores- tiny sea creatures that lived in the sea millions of years ago. In fact about 90 million years ago! They do not exist today so no chalk stone is being formed anymore.

fensive structure at the entrance to Shoreham harbour. Originally it would have been armed with six 68 pounder guns. The 1st Sussex Volunteer Artillery, one of the best, were stationed here. It was used in World War II with searchlights and two 6-inch guns.

Near Brighton

Devil's Dyke

Near Brighton, West Sussex,
Tel: 01273 857712
www.nationaltrust.org.uk/devils-dyke
It is just 5 miles north of Brighton, and has a spectacular view from the top. Legend has it the Devil dug the valley to drown the people below. However we know that the very steep slope in the north side formed in the Ice Age. The bank is an Iron Age earthwork, and is a mile long. It is the largest dry valley in England.
Getting there: Bus 77 from Rottingdean

Saddlescombe Farm and Newtimber Hill

Saddlescombe Road, near Brighton, West Sussex, BN45 7DE
Tel: 01273 857712
saddlescombe@nationaltrust.org.uk

www.nationaltrust.org.uk/saddlescombe-farm-and-newtimber-hill
The farm is over 450 acres and can be found in the Domesday Book. Some believe it to have once been home to the Knights Templar. It is a traditional sheep, cow and arable farm. You can visit the farm and try being a shepherd for the day for £175 per family, contact them on 01273 857062 or 07776 393072. This would need to be booked ahead.

Newtimber Hill is a good example of chalk grassland in the country. It is next to the farm and has good views of the sea and the South Downs. In early autumn, the hill is covered in a purple blanket of Devil's bit scabious. The north face of the hill is an ancient woodland, where you can find beech trees with graffiti dating back to 1880.
Getting there: BUS 13X bus. Runs hourly Eastbourne Terminus Road to Brighton via Birling Gap

Further Afield

Black Down

Tennyson's Lane, Haslemere, Surrey GU27
Tel: 01428 652359
blackdown@nationaltrust.org.uk

Photo by Jason Long

www.nationaltrust.org.uk/black-down

The highest point in the South Downs National Park, and it has a wild feel to it. There are flower meadows, purple heather and pine trees. There are ancient sunken lanes and drove ways where shepherds would have herded their sheep to market. Now there are occasional cows to feed on the brush. One of Britain's rarest butterflies, the Silver-studded Blue, is being reintroduced on land at Black Down.

Queen Elizabeth Country Park

Gravel Hill, Horndean, Waterlooville, Hampshire PO8 0QE
Tel: 023 9259 5040
www3.hants.gov.uk/qecp

It is one of the furthest parts of the Downs from Brighton, but is a beautiful park. This is a huge place with 2,000 acres of open access woodland and land set within the South Downs National Park. The Butser Hill National Nature Reserve is within the site. If you are lucky you can spot deer in the extensive beech woods. There are 20 miles of trails for walker, cyclists and horse riders. It has an Adventure Play trail for the over 8s, and animal themed playground for the smaller children. It has been voted one of the nation's favourite parks.

Slindon Estate

Top Road, Slindon, near Arundel, West Sussex, BN18 0RG
Tel: 01243 814730
www.nationaltrust.org.uk/slindon-estate

Slindon Estate is 1,400 hectares of woodland, downland, farmland, parkland and an unspoilt Sussex village. The village is worth a potter. There are also more than 40km of rights of way that criss-cross the estate. In spring, there are wonderful woodland flowers, bluebells in the village and on Nore Hill and a lambing event at Gaston Farm. In summer, walk in the shady woodland lanes up through the estate. Stane Street is a three mile Roman road. Find the medieval deer bank 'park pale' which surrounds the old deer park.

The Long Man of Wilmington

The Street, Wilmington, Polegate, East Sussex, BN26 5SL
http://sussexpast.co.uk/properties-to-discover/the-long-man
The giant man is 235 feet high. It is a mystery as to the origins of the Long Man. Some believed that it was made by monks. Others that it is from the 16th or 17th Century. There is one theory that if it was built in 3500BC it would have marked the constellation Orion's movement across the ridge. This would make it from Neolithic times. In World War II it was painted green to prevent air planes using it as a landmark.

For a long time it was only a shadow in the grass, visible after a snow fall. The head could have been a helmet shape, which gives strength to the theory that the figure is a helmeted war-god.

The South Downs Way

www.nationaltrail.co.uk/south-downs-way
All the way from Winchester, the first capital of England, and the white chalk cliffs at Eastbourne. It is 100 miles to walk all the way. There are three sections around Brighton and down to the picturesque cliffs, that are briefly described here.

River Adur to River Ouse - 21 miles (33.8 Km)

This path takes you through Devil's Dyke, Saddlescombe Farm, the Jack & Jill Windmills, the traditional 'Dew Ponds' and up to Ditchling Beacon. At 248m this is the highest point along the Sussex Downs and is often a good spot for an ice cream from the van at the car park. From here a bus service runs back to Brighton. Alternatively, you can carry on the path to the outskirts of Lewes, and downwards to the River Ouse and the village of Southease.

River Ouse to River Cuckmere & Alfriston - 7 miles (11.3 Km)

At the bottom of the Itford Hill, see if you can see any seals in the water, apparently they like to visit! There is a climb up the long Itford Hill. You wont pass a single tree until you reach Alfriston! The views are very open and on a clear day, can be spectacular. The path goes on past Firle Beacon, and on to Cuckmere and Alfriston.

Alfriston to Eastbourne via Seven Sisters -10.5 miles (16.9 Km)

At Alfristion the route splits into two routes, one just a footpath, the other for cyclists and horse-riders also. These rejoin at Eastbourne so you could make loop back if you so wished. The route follows the River Cuckmere south, though Friston Forest and then into Seven Sisters Country Park, down to the coast and then up and down the seven cliffs.

Between Cuckmere Haven and Beachy Head, the path is very steep up and down, so only take this route if you are able, and probably not suitable for smaller children. The cliffs are also undercut and unprotected so don't get too close to the edge!

South Downs National Park Authority Learning Zone

A great website all about the downs, the geology, the landscapes, culture and heritage.
http://learning.southdowns.gov.uk

"You can see Lewes lying like a box of toys under a great amphitheatre of chalk hills ... on the whole it is set down better than any town I have seen in England".

William Morris (1834-1896)

A very pretty town snuggled in the Ouse valley of the South Downs. It is just a few miles from Brighton and well linked by train and bus. It has some great shops for kids clothes, nice cafes, parks and walks along the river and onto the Downs.

Lewes has 10 twittens, old Saxon lanes, one of which is Keere Street. There is a Russian Memorial (1877) honouring prisoners captured during the Crimean War and the Martyrs Memorial (1901) to commemorate the 17 protestant martyrs burned at the stake in Lewes High Street. The Pells Pool, built in 1860, is the oldest freshwater lido in England.

There are some nice, gentle walks from Lewes. You can walk over Mount Caburn to the village of Glynde, or wander up to Lewes Brooks the RSPB reserve. The South Downs Way skirts around Lewes. The pretty village of Kingston near Lewes is accessible from Southover. Or follow the river Ouse to Hamsey Place from the Pells.

For eating out, there are a couple of great Italian restaurants, and some nice cafes. And if it's raining there is always the Leisure Centre for swimming or softplay.

Attractions

Anne of Cleves House Museum

52, Southover High St, Lewes, BN7 1JA
Tel: 01273 474610
www.sussexpast.co.uk

A lovely example of a 15th century timber-framed house in Lewes. It was part of Queen Anne's annulment settlement from King Henry VIII in 1541, although she never stayed there. It has been furnished to look as it would have been in Queen Anne's time. Plus there is Sussex pottery and an ironwork gallery. Special events are held for children.

Open: Summer 10.00am to 5.00pm
Winter 10.00am to 4.00pm
Note: 11.00am opening on Sundays, Mondays and Bank Holidays.

Admission: Adult £5.20, child £2.90, concessions £4.80, family £14.00 (1 adult and 4 children, or 2 adults and 2 children).

Bulls House

92, High Street, Lewes, BN7 1XH
Tel: 01273 486260

The house is not generally open to the public, but tours of the house can be booked at the weekend with local historic tour guide Mary Burke.

Barbican House Museum

169, High Street, Lewes, BN7 1YE Tel: 01273 486290
http://sussexpast.co.uk/properties-to-discover/anne-of-cleves-house

Bentley Wildfowl and Motor Museum

Halland, Lewes, BN8 5AF
Tel: 01825 840573
www.bentley.org.uk

Edwardian and vintage cars and motorcycles at this iconic stately home. There is an interactive trail which makes discovering the wildlife fun. There is also an adventure playground, picnic area and cafe.

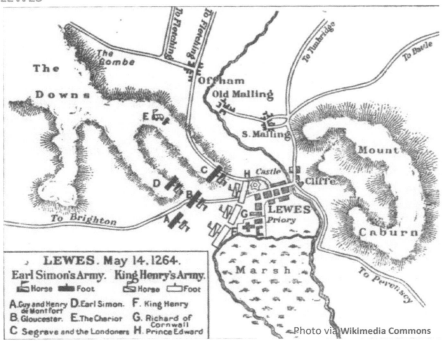

LEWES. May 14. 1264.
Earl Simon's Army. King Henry's Army.
Horse Foot Horse Foot
A. Guy and Henry de Montfort D. Earl Simon. F. King Henry
B. Gloucester. E. The Chariot G. Richard of Cornwall
C. Segrave and the Londoners H. Prince Edward

Photo via Wikimedia Commons

The Battle of Lewes

William de Warenne, 1st Earl of Surry was given the land of Lewes. He built Lewes Castle. It was the site of a mint during the late Anglo-Saxon period. The Battle of Lewes took place in the fields just west of Landport. Here Henry III forces lost to Simon de Monfort in 1264.

Michelham Priory

Michelham Priory, Upper Dicker, Hailsham, East Sussex, BN27 3QS
Tel: 01323 844224
http://sussexpast.co.uk/properties-to-discover/michelham-priory
The Priory is the site of a former Augustine Priory, dating from the 13th century. The Priory was dissolved in 1537 with the dissolution of the monasteries by Henry VIII, and the Church demolished after. It has seven acres of grounds, a medieval herb garden, a working watermill and forge. It has a children's play area and trails.
Admission: Adult £7.80, Child (5-15) £4.20

The Round House

A formed windmill in Pipe Passage was owned by the writer Virginia Woolf, however she never lived here.

Lewes Leisure Centre

Mountfield Road, Lewes, BN7 2XG
Tel: 01273 486000
www.waveleisure.co.uk/leisure centres/lewes-leisure-centre.html
Lewes Leisure Centre has two swimming pools, a 25m large pool, a sauna and a small family pool. It is very near the railway station. The centre offers special family fun sessions with large floats, usually on Saturdays and Sundays. It also offers free swimming sessions for children during the school holidays.

The leisure centre also has a soft play area and provides the following activities for children: football, gymnastics, badminton, short tennis, street dance, trampolining and supervised climbing. Thursdays from 10-11.30 drop-in parent and toddler group.

Ocean Adventure Indoor Play Area - Lewes Leisure Centre

www.waveleisure.co.uk/lewes-leisure-centre/ocean-adventure
This is a soft play area over three levels for children under 8. You can slide down the sea serpent and climb through seaweed and octopus tentacles.

Art & Galleries

Hop Gallery

Found within the former Star Brewery in Market Street

St Anne's Gallery

This is in the High Street and has occasional art exhibitions.

The Foundry Gallery

This was converted by Artemis Arts from the former Market Lane Garage.

Lewes Film Club

Tel: 01273 483550
www.lewes-filmclub.com
Film showings are in the All Saints Centre, a former church. It has a junior film club, set up to introduce young people to classic films and world cinema. Films are usually at 2pm on the last Sunday of each month, tickets £4 child, £5 adults.

Glyndebourne opera house

Founded in 1934, the venue draws large audiences for its Summer Festival and has attracted a host of international talent throughout its history.

Sculpture in Lewes

Eric Gill, John Kelton, Joseph Cribb and William Rothenstein are just some of the notable figures who have lived and worked in Lewes. The Helmet (1964), by Enzo Plazzotta is in the grounds of Lewes Priory. The Cuilfail Spiral (1983) by Peter Randall-Page sits on the roundabout at the north

Lewes Castle & Museum

Lewes Castle photo via **Wikimedia Commons**

169 High Street, Lewes, BN7 1YE
Tel: 01273 486290
www.sussexpast.co.uk

A 1000 year old Norman Castle which stands at the highest point of Lewes. If you make the long climb to the top you can see all around the Sussex Downs. The Barbican house museum next door has the history of the castle and the area.

It is built on a mound artificially created with chalk. Originally it was called Bray Castle. It has two mottes, which are the defensive ditches to protect from attack. There is only one other monument in England with similar mottes, in Lincoln. The Castle was built by William de Wrenne, 1st Earl of Surrey and son-in-law of William the Conqueror.

Open: November to February: 10 am to 3.45 pm. March to October: 10 am to 5.30 pm. Open at 11 am on Sundays, Mondays and Bank holidays.
Admission: Adult £7.00, Child (5-15) £3.60, Concessions £6.40, Family £18.80 (1 adult and 4 children, or 2 adults and 2 children)

end of the Cuilfail Tunnel. It is made of 7 pieces of Portland limestone. The Magnus Inscription (c.1200)on the East wall of St John Sub Castro. The Janus Head (1997) by John Skelton and Lewes Group (2010) by Jon Edgar are in Southover Grange Gardens.

Events

Children's Patina Moving On Parade - July

www.patinalewes.com
In 2014 320 children from 14 schools took part in the film themed carnival style parade.

FestivalArtWave - Aug/Sep

www.artwavefestival.org
A visual arts festival held over three weekends every August and September.

Lewes Folk Festival - October

www.lewesfolkfest.org
Dance, folk and song festival over two days in October.

Lewes Bonfire Night

Town Centre, 5th November
This is a huge event in Lewes and the biggest bonfire night in the country. Guy Fawkes Night, on 5 November marks the uncovering of the Gunpowder Plot in 1605 to blow up the houses of Parliament. The event in Lewes is bigger as it also commemorates the 17 Protestant martyrs burnt at the stake in the 16th Century. They are controversial as they involve burning an effigy of the Pope.

Lewes Tourist Information

187 High St, Lewes, East Sussex BN7 2DE
Tel: 01273 483448
Email: lewes.tic@lewes.gov.uk
www.lewes.gov.uk

Opening Hours
1 April to 30 September

The Pells Outdoor Swimming Pool

Pells Pool photo via **Wikimedia Commons**

Brook Street, Lewes, BN7 2BA
thepellspool@yahoo.co.uk
Tel: 01273 472334
www.pellspool.org.uk

The outdoor pool in Lewes is the oldest and one of the largest freshwater pools in the country. It was originally donated to the Constables and townspeople of the town in May 1603. There is also a children's paddling pool, sunbathing terrace and a cafe. The terrace is on a tree lined lawn, perfect for summer days. It is open from May to September. Recent excavations show that the present pool tank, lies within two previous shells. The oldest is an original brick-lined pool.

Admission: 2013 Prices: Adult £4; Junior and Concessions £2; Family (2 adults and 2 children) £10.50 Children under 2 go free.

Monday to Saturday: 9:30am - 4:30pm

Sundays and Bank Holidays: 10:00am - 2:00pm
1 October to 31 March

Monday to Friday: 9:30am - 4:30pm (Closed from 12:00-1:00pm)

Saturday: 10:00am - 2:00pm

Sundays and Bank Holidays: Closed

Eating Out

Jolly Sportsman
East Chiltington
Tel: 01273 890400
www.thejollysportsman.com
A lovely garden, a children's play area, and a great menu from chef Richard Willis. Try the gorgeous slow cooked lamb, herbs from their own garden, or sorbet of elderflower. Mains from £13.25.

Vrac
18 Lansdown Place, Lewes BN7 2JT
Tel: 01273 476696
A great selection of teas, especially if you like ethical and herbal varieties. Lovely small cakes too.

From the Hearth
Eastgate, Opposite Waitrose, Lewes BN7 2LP
Tel: 01273 470755
Not the most glamorous of locations, but the food is fantastic. A great choice of pizzas made with their own sour dough on the premises.

Famiglia Lazzati
17 Market Street, Lewes BN7 2NB
Tel: 01273 479539
A small restaurant stylishly decorated serving a good choice of Italian food. There is a fixed price £10 lunch which is a good deal. Great for all the family.

The Cock Inn
Uckfield Road, Ringmer, Lewes BN8 5RX
Tel: 01273 812040
Fantastic roasts, which are huge! Good children's food, plain and local. It is a bit out of town but just by the main road so good as a stopping off point.

Lewes Train Station 1920s
via Wikimedia Commons

Pocket history of Lewes

There were prehistoric dwellers in Lewes. The Roman settlement of Mutuantonis was also thought to be in the area.

After the Norman invasion of England in 1066, William de Warenne made it his domain. The tombs of William and his wife Gundrada are now in the St John the Baptist Church. He built Lewes Castle.

For hundreds of years it was the main legal and administrative centre of Sussex. In the 16th Century, Henry VIII dissolved the monasteries which led to Lewes Priory being demolished.

In the mid 16th century Lewes was the site of the execution of 17 Protestant martyrs, burned at the stake in front of the Star Inn (now the Town Hall).

In 1836, an avalanche of snow from the cliff dropped on a row of cottages in South Street and 8 people died. The Snowdrop pub is named in memory of this event.
Sourced from article: http://en.wikipedia.org/wiki/Lewes

Famous residents of Lewes

Tom Paine (1737-1809) - Founding father of the American War of Independence and the French Revolution.
Dame Grace Kimmins (1871-1954) - Social activist.
Hugh Harris - Guitarist with The Kooks
Polly Toynbee - Journalist and writer.
Virginia Woolf (1882-1941) - Novelist.
William McCrea (1904-1999) - discovered that the sun was mostly hydrogen.

OUT & ABOUT IN SUSSEX TOWNS

The South East in and around Sussex is a wonderful place to take day trips, short breaks or longer stay at home holidays. From the Art Deco seafront hotels in Worthing, to homely B&Bs on the Downs, to chic hotels in Brighton.

If you like camping or caravanning there are a great variety of camp sites, some quiet and peaceful, others with all the amenities. The seaside and the picturesque rolling South Downs stretch across Sussex to Eastbourne. Chichester, Arundel, Hastings and Lewes. They are all packed full of activities for kids. Set their imagination alight with castles and tales of medieval knights, at Arundel, Hastings or Bodiam.

Photo by Tirza van Dijk

Kingley Vale is a wonderful ancient forest, with some of the oldest Yew trees in the country. It is a great place for picnics, and kids can pretend they are in a fairytale with the twisted roots of trees.

You can also take the young ones to pet lambs or little pigs at the many open farms. Learn about the Romans in Britain by immersing your children in the wonderful Roman Palace at Fishbourne. Many of these are listed in the chapter on Sussex attractions, pages 61-64 , and wildlife and farms pages 40-42.

There are steam railways, bluebell walks, country parks for kicking about leaves in the Autumn, and great fish and chip shops to round off a day rock pooling.

Alfriston

A pretty town in the valley of the river Cuckmere. The first building of the National Trust was acquired here - the Clergy House. Alfriston Festival is in the week before August Bank Holiday Weekend. It has a traditional village fair on the Tye, the local village green.

Battle of Hastings Renactment via Wikimedia Commons

The family friendly Fishers Farm Park is nearby.

The Weald and Downland Open Air Museum

This has over 45 historic buildings, rebuilt in a parkland setting with woodland walks, Shire horses, and a 17th century mill. There's a soft play area for tots.

Amazing Maize Maze

Tulleys Farm near Crawley (summer holidays only). Over three miles over an area of five acres. One of the largest and most intricate puzzles in the world.

The George

Alfriston
Tel: 01323 870 319
A historic pub, from 1397, serves good fresh and local food. Mains from £9.95.

Arundel

The gothic Cathedral and Arundel Castle, seat of The Dukes of Norfolk, are the first impressions of Arundel, as they tower above the town. The place is also near the South Downs and the river Arun. It has a victorian centre full of antique shops and art galleries. A Farmers Market takes place on the 3rd Saturday of each month. The Arundel Wetland Centre, 26 hectares of naturalised landscape is nearby. Arundel Lido is a good outdoor pool in the summer.

St Nicholas Parish Church

Built in 1380, this is the only church in England to house both Anglican and Roman Catholic Churches under the same roof.

Chichester

This used to the capital of Sussex, and has many historic buildings, such as the cathedral. It is 900 years old, with medieval carvings and a Victorian spire. Goodwood House nearby is owned by the Duke of Richmond, nad is one of the finest stately homes in the country. Petworth House is a majestic mansion within a huge landscaped park, full of deer.

Kingley Vale

West Stoke, Chichester
This fairy tale wood can be found half a mile on a level track from the free car parking area at West Stoke. There are some steep climbs if you want to take in the views, over the Bronze Age barrows known as "The Devil's Humps". It is great for a picnic spot. There are even 300 year old Yew trees. There is a grove of ancient trees which are among the oldest living things in Britain. The reserve is also an important archaeological site.

Eastbourne

Right next to Beachy Head and the spectacular white cliffs, it has five theatres and award winning beaches. Every year it has a free airshow that you can see from the seafront. Or see the Magnificent Motors or Extreme Sports festivals. Fort Fun has a log flume and lots of water and adventure fun. Nearby Drusillas Park offers a winning combination of animals, adventure play areas and Thomas the Tank Engine.

Forest Row

Ashdown Forest is nearby and is where Winnie the Pooh was created. It began life as a small hamlet, popular with noblemen who liked hunting deer in the 14th century. The Forest Way Country Park is also nearby. Ashdown Llama Park, Chiddingstone Castle and the Bluebell Railway are all attractions.

Hastings

The unmistakable black fishing huts on Hasting's seafront and Britain's steepest funicular railway are part of the quirkiness of this seaside place. It is most famous for being where William the Conqueror landed in 1066. Did you know it is also the birthplace of television? Invented by John Logie Baird in 1923.

It has a Coastal Currents Arts Festival, and a recently opened University Centre. The seafront has interesting light installations of marine monolith 'Stream' and 'Sticks of Rock'. The area also has a great 660 acre Hastings Country Park, with clifftop views. For

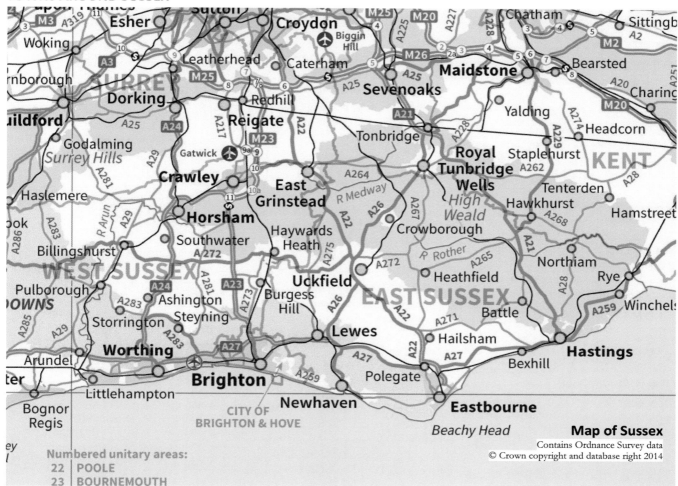

Map of Sussex

Contains Ordnance Survey data
© Crown copyright and database right 2014

Numbered unitary areas:
22 POOLE
23 BOURNEMOUTH

activities try the Smugglers Adventure Park, the the Sealife centre.

Smugglers Adventure

St Clement's Caves, Hastings, TN34 3HY.
Tel: 01424 422964
www.smugglersadventure.co.uk
A warren of caves and caverns was discovered by Joseph Golding, a greengrocer who was asked to cut a garden seat into the side of the cliff. When his pick went through the rock, he found a maze of tunnels. The caves have been an attraction since the Victorian years. Smugglers traded into-bacco, leather, tea and spices. There is also a rumour has it the caves are Haunted!

Blue Reef Aquarium

Rock-A-Nore Road, Hastings, East Sussex. TN34 3DW
Tel: 0844 549 9088
www.bluereefaquarium.co.uk
A short walk away in the historic old town is the Blue Reef Aquarium. Crabs, seahorses and sharks prowl. There is even a giant ocean tank with an underwater tunnel.

Hastings Castle

Castle Hill Rd, Hastings, East Sussex TN34 3QZ
www.visit1066country.com/attractions/history/castles
Hastings Castle is a huge part of England's history as it was the first Norman motte and bailey castle to be built here. William the Conqueror, landed in England in 1066, and ordered Hast-
ings Castle to be built. William went on to defeat King Harold II at the Battle of Hastings at a site close to the town of Battle. In World War II, Hastings was heavily bombed and an anti-aircraft gun was placed outside the Castle's East Wall for protection.

Bluebells Cafe Tearoom

87 High Street, Battle TN33 0AQ
Traditional teas and lovely cakes.

Di Polas

14 Marine Parade, Hastings
A really good ice-cream parlour, perfect for mouth watering flavours on a hot sunny day.

Maggie's

Rock-a-Nore Road, Hastings TN34 3DW

59

The best fish and chips, some say, with great large portions and properly cooked delicious chips.

Soul Food

3 George Street, Hastings TN34 3EG
In the old town of Hastings, this small restaurant serves up great soul food, from jerk chicken to curry.

Haywards Heath

This is one of the larger town, with good commercial shopping and links to London. Victoria Park is the town's main open space and has an adventure playground. Beech Hurst Gardens has a playground and a miniature railway.

The High Weald

This is, like the South Downs, an area of natural beauty. It is a medieval landscape with ancient droveways and rolling hills. Ashdown Forest is open heathland and woodland on the highest sandy ridge-top of the High Weald. It is the Hundred Acre Wood inspiration for Winnie the Pooh, by A.A. Milne.

Horsham

The historic town of Horsham has twittens and passageways, and some good markets on Thursday and Saturdays. The Pavilions in the Park swimming and leisure complex has a children's indoor adventure play area, swimming pools and a flume ride.

Nearby, the Warnham Nature Reserve is 92 acres of forest and country and has 150 species of bird life. Great romantic poet Percy Shelley was born on the outskirts of the town at Warnham.

Rye

Perched on a hill, the medieval town of Rye is small but evocative of times gone by. It used to be the sea! How ever the waves have retreated two miles south.

The historic centre is the Citadel on a rocky outcrop. It is here you'll find the Church of St Mary the Virgin. On Lion Street there is a clock from 1561. Explore the cobbled streets and see the Ypres Tower and Landgate Arch. Mermaid Street has houses with strange names; 'The House Opposite' and 'The House with the Seat'. Henry James, the author, used to live in Lamb House.

Knoops

Tower Forge, Hilders Cliff, Landgate, Rye TN31 7LD
A chocolate lovers paradise, this small little cafe has an amazing array of cocoa filled goodies. You can have small tasters. It also serves the most delicious hot chocolate. Your kids will love you!

Worthing

This has a lovely long promenade, with Palm trees and gardens, and a good pier. There is sand at low tide. Along the pier you can look back and see the Seven Sisters. You can still buy fresh fish straight from the fisherman on the beach. Attractions include Highdown Gardens and Brooklands Park. In 1894, Oscar Wilde wrote The Importance of Being Earnest at No 5, The Esplanade.

Every year there is the Worthing Birdman Competition - where contestants compete to fly!

Sussex Tourist Information Centres

Tourist Information Centres are useful places to find information, maps and books.

Arundel	01903 882456
Battle & Bexhill	01424 776789
Brighton	03003 000088
Burgess Hill	01444 238202
Chichester	01243 775888
Eastbourne	0871 663 0031
East Grinstead	01342 410121
Hastings	01424 451111
Horsham	01403 211661
Lewes	01273 483448
Littlehampton	01903 718984
Midhurst	01798 812251
Rye	01797 229049
Seaford	01323 897426
Worthing	01903 221066

Also worth checking are these websites:
www.lovesussex.com - what's on in Sussex
www.sussextourism.org.uk - top attractions

ANIMALS & WILDLIFE

Wildlife Parks

Arundel Wildfowl and Wetlands Centre
Mill Road, Arundel, BN18 9PB
Tel: 01903 883355
www.wwt.org.uk/visit-us/arundel
A specialist wetland conservation centre owned by The Wildfowl & Wetlands Trust. It provides a home to a variety of wildlife, such as ducks, geese and swans, and is a fun and interesting place to learn about nature. Café, gift shop, picnic area.

Ashdown Forest Llama Park
Wych Cross, Forest Row, RH18 5JN
Tel: 01825 712040
www.llamapark.co.uk
There are over 100 llamas and alpacas on this 30 acre park. Farm trail (suitable for buggies), adventure play area, museum, picnic area, café, gift shop.

Bentley Wildfowl and Motor Museum
Halland, Lewes, BN8 5AF
Tel: 01825 840573
www.bentley.org.uk
Over 1000 swans, geese and ducks as well as veteran, Edwardian and vintage cars and motorcycles can be found at this stunning stately home. An interactive trail makes learning about the wildlife fun. Adventure playground, picnic area, café, gift shop. There are also rabbits, Kune Kune pigs and lambs in the spring.

Drusillas Park
Alfriston Road, Afriston, BN26 5QS
Tel: 01323 874100
www.drusillas.co.uk
Drusillas Park is widely regarded as the best small zoo in Europe and was voted 2010/2011 South East England's Visitor Attraction of the Year. Enjoy a fun finding-out day out that includes Thomas the Tank Engine and brilliant play areas! Free Animal Spotter Book when you arrive. Hello Kitty Secret Garden - which includes a specially designed Hello Kitty car ride, a tea cup ride and a "reach for the sky" hopper ride Babies under 2 go free, a family of 2 is from £21 to £29 (online price).

Earnley Butterflies Birds and Beasts
133 Almodington Lane, Earnley, Chichester PO20 7JR
Tel: 01243 512637
www.earnleybutterfliesandgardens.co.uk
Tropical butterflies, exotic birds, covered theme gardens, play area, crazy golf (extra charge), café, shop, picnic area. Reptiles, raptors, donkeys and many small animals you can feed. Only open in the summer months.

Huxley Birds of Prey Experience
Falcon Lodge, Sedgwick Lane, Brighton Road, Horsham, RH13 6QD
Tel: 01403 273458
www.flyingfalcons.co.uk
Meet over 70 different birds and watch the owl display. A beautiful garden with a Japanese water feature.

Noah's Ark Animal & Reptile Rescue
133 Almodington Lane, Earnley, Chichester PO20 7JR
Tel: 01243 512637
www.noahs-ark.freeuk.com
Home to nearly 400 small animals, tortoises and reptiles that have been rescued after being abandoned, neglected or injured.

Seven Sisters Sheep Centre
Gilberts Drive, East Dean, East Sussex BN20 0AA
Tel: 01323 423207
www.sheepcentre.co.uk
Children can get involved at this family run farm, where there are over 50 different breeds of sheep. Meet and feed the lambs and other animals

including pigs, goats, rabbits and chicks. Take a tractor ride. Have a real Sussex cream tea in the tea room. Prices : Adult £ 6.00 O.A.P £ 5.50; Child £ 5.00; Family £21.00

Farms

Blackberry Farm
Whitesmith, Nr Lewes, BN8 6JD
Tel: 01825 872912
www.blackberry-farm.co.uk
There are animal handling sessions, pony and tractor rides,and a play area, cafe and shop. It is set in 18 acres of beautiful Sussex countryside in the village of Whitesmith and home to over 200 animals. Clucky's indoor adventure play area and has a wall of mirrors, zip wires and chasm swing. It

Did you Know?
- A domestic dog is a subspecies of the gray wolf. They have a sense of smell up to 1 million times more sensitive than humans.
- Polar bears share DNA of Irish Brown Bears and are probably descended from Ireland.
- Pigeons can learn to tell the difference between Monet and Picasso.
- A bee must travel the equivalent of 3x around the world to produce one jar of honey. They also have 5 eyes.
- A snail can sleep for 3 years.
- Ants will not cross a chalk line.
- For every person there are about 200 million insects.
- The hedgehog likes to eat slugs, worms and beetles.

Information from wikipaedia.com

Nature web sites for kids
canalrivertrust.org.uk/explorers/families
www.rspb.org.uk
www.wildlifewatch.org.uk
www.naturedetectives.org.uk

also has a toddler zone, baby and flat zone.

Coombes Farm
Lancing, BN15 0RS
Tel: 01273 452028
www.coombes.co.uk
Farm tours on tractors and trailers over the south downs and around the farm. Visit in lambing season when over 1000 lambs are born.

Fishers Farm Park
Newpound Lane, Wisborough Green, West Sussex RH14 0EG
Tel: 01403 700063
www.fishersfarmpark.co.uk
Award winning adventure play attraction and farm open all year. Pony and tractor rides, climbing wall, crazy golf, bumper boats, barn theatre, indoor play areas, restaurant, special events, gift shop.

Gaston Farm
School Hill, Slindon, BN18 0RS
Tel: 01243 814269
www.gastonfarm.com
Open for lambing season throughout April.

Heaven Farm
Furners Green, Uckfield, BN22 3RG
Tel: 01825 790226
www.heavenfarm.co.uk
Open all year. Nature trail, farm museum, farm shop, craft shop. Camping & caravanning.

Holmbush Farm World
Crawley Road, Faygate, Nr Horsham, RH12 4SE
Tel: 01293 851110
www.holmbushfarm.co.uk
Tractor rides, animal handling, animal barns, play areas (including indoor) and picnic areas.

Middle Farm
Firle, nr Lewes, BN8 6LJ
Tel: 01323 811411
www.middlefarm.com

Open 7 days a week. A welcoming working farm for all the family to enjoy. Restaurant and farm shop.

Spring Barn Farm
Kingston Road, Lewes BN7 3ND
info@springbarnfarm.com
Tel: 01273 488 450
www.springbarnfarm.com
This has an indoor and outdoor play area. It also has slides, pedal tractors, go karts and jumping pillows. There are animals too for the children to see. There are under 5s and 3s soft play areas. You can also help feed the pigs!

Tulleys Farm
Turners Hill Road, Turners Hill, Crawley, RH10 4PE
Tel: 01342 718472
www.tulleysfarm.com
Family run farm which is open daily. Play areas, mini diggers and tractors, seasonal events, such as Easter egg hunt and a giant maize maze! Tea rooms.

Washbrooks Farm
Brighton Road, Hurstpierpoint BN6 9EF
Tel: 01273 832201
www.washbrooks.co.uk
Open 7 days a week. A family run farm catering for families with young children up to 8 years old. Meet the animals, indoor and outdoor play areas, special events, tea room. Child £6.50, Adult £7.50

Seagulls, foxes, butterflies and birds

Local wildlife is great to spot. The Downs countryside is the place to see wallows and swifts nesting in old eaves. If you are lucky you will see in the dusk bats hunting for insects and badgers exploring. The wildflowers include violets, primroses, wood anemones and bluebells. There are greater spotted woodpeckers, green woodpeckers, bullfinch, goldfinch, chaffinch and greenfinch gather in open woods.

There are hidden families of foxes. I once saw a whole family in Hollingbury right by a bus stop. Urban seagulls are easier to spot, and can be very loud! They are protected by the Wildlife and Country Act and it is offence to remove or harm their eggs.

Sussex Wildlife Trust

www.sussexwildlifetrust.org.uk
The trust conserves the many wildlife species around the coast, woodlands and countryside. It also runs courses and invites volunteers on projects.

Nature Tots

They run popular 'Nature Tot' for 3-5 year olds - pre-school woodland experiences for a small fee. Held at Woods Mill nature reserve near Henfield, Seven Sisters Country Park near Seaford and Tilgate Park near Crawley. All children must be accompanied by an adult. Expect to get a bit muddy so wear appropriate clothing for the weather!
Example in 2014:
Seven Sisters Country Park
Family Members: £7.50 for two weeks
Non Members: £8.50 for two weeks

Brighton and Hove Youth Rangers (16 - 25)
Brighton and Hove Wildlife Rangers (12 - 16)

People and Wildlife Officer (Brighton)
Tel: 01273 290393
In school holidays, join the rangers groups and identify and learn about wildlife. Carry out practical conservation tasks to improve habitats. Survey and monitor plants and animals. Garden for wildlife. Country crafts. Nature photography. Weekly sessions run from 10.00 – 15.00.
Cost: £10 per person per session

Nature by Season

Spring
This is nest building time for birds, see if you can spot them in the trees. Listen to the bird songs, cuckoos, woodpeckers, pigeons, blackbirds and crows. Find frogspawn in ponds, and see the catkins, blossom, bluebells and daffodils bloom.

Summer
Look out for ants, see how they follow a trail and carry leaves many times bigger than themselves. Bees and cabbage white butterflies are hovering around the flowers. Yellow dandelions, daisies and buttercups are on the meadows. On a hot day in the grass, you may be able to hear grasshoppers. Ladybirds help to eat the green aphids which attack plants.

Autumn
A great time to go on acorn, conker and pine cone hunts, and run through russet red fallen leaves. Squirrels will be collecting for their winter store. Spiders and their webs are comon. There are also mushrooms growing in grasslands and around trees.

Winter
See which trees and bushes have lost their leaves, and which are evergreen, like holly, ivy and pines. Hedgehogs and bats hibernate, other animals have to find shelter.

SPORTS, ARTS & ACTIVITIES FOR CHILDREN

This section contains information on local activities; sports, swimming, arts, drama, music and more in the Brighton area. There are so many activities that your child could join to develop their athletic talents, fitness and creativity. There are also general groups like the Girl Guides or the Scouts. Most indoor pools offer swimming lessons, and the area is well serviced with sports centres.

Brighton and Hove Scouts - not just for boys

www.brightonandhovescouts.org.uk
From 6 years To 25 years
Provides adventure and personal development opportunities for young people aged 6-25. Over 400,000 young people in the UK are in the scouts. It was started over a 100 years ago and is still go-ing strong today. You can join your local group for a fee of between £50 to £100 a year to cover facilities and costs. The emphasis is on fun and adventure, building confidence and friendships.

There are badges and awards in hiking, healthy eating, camping, IT, mechanics and more. Children can join from aged 6, with the Beaver Scouts. They usually meet weekly to take part in games, crafts, singing, good turns. Cub scouts are from 8-10, then Scouts. As well as weekly meetings, there are chances to have holidays and camps with adventure activities.

Girl Guides

Join Girlguiding: Register your interest or call on 0800 1 69 59 01.
General enquiries: 020 7834 6242
www.girlguiding-anglia.org.uk
www.girlguiding.org.uk

The girl guide association is a charity where girls can meet up locally, and under the supervision of volunteer leaders, can build friendships, learn life skills and have fun. Rainbows are for girls aged 5 to 7, Browies from 7 to 10 who become a member of a six and follow a programme called 'Brownie Adventure'. Guides are from 10 to 14 and try out activities from adventure sports to performing arts or community action projects. There is also a senior section from 14 to 26 years.

NOTE:
Please check the details, by website or by phone before you go to any activity. Whilst the author has tried to ensure that these are as accurate as possible, they are subject to change.

If you're looking for some fun activities in the countryside around Brighton & Hove, we've got some great ideas.

For activity lovers, learning to climb a tree with Climbing Wild is lots of fun, whilst thrill seekers can take to the skies with Brighton Scenic for stunning views across the Sussex downs & coast.

SPORTS & SWIMMING

Indoor Swimming Pools

Swimming is a great activity for kids, promoting confidence, physical ability and a whole lot of fun. Brighton and Hove residents under the age of 16 can swim for free during public swimming sessions at the King Alfred, Prince Regent and St Luke's. All the pools listed here give swimming lessons for all ages. Some also host birthday pool parties and junior fun sessions.

Prince Regent Swimming Complex

Church Street Brighton BN1 1YA
Tel: 01273 685692
www.freedom-leisure.co.uk

Right in the city centre, this has a main pool of 25 metres long. It has a teaching pool for families with small children. The shallow pool with adjacent water slide is open after school and during school holidays.

It has also has a gym, a sauna and a steam room.

Amongst the classes on offer are aqua natal for new and expectant mothers and a parent and child workout.

There is a supervised non-registered crèche, available on Tuesday, Thursday and Friday mornings. Check in advance to book.

King Alfred Leisure Centre

Kingsway, Hove BN3 2WW
Tel: 01273 290290
www.freedom-leisure.co.uk

This has a pool, gym and studio and has recently been improved. The pool is 25 metres long with a children's play area and a separate teaching pool.

The gym has been recently refurbished with the latest fitness kit. Classes include spin, Zumba, Body Combat, yoga, antenatal yoga and more. There is a sports hall for badminton, table tennis, indoor 5 a side, and martial arts. Every Sunday a roller disco is held in the Sports Hall. It also has a ballroom and an indoor Bowls hall.

St Luke's Swimming Pool

St Luke's Terrace, Brighton BN2 9ZE
Tel: 01273 602385
www.freedom-leisure.co.uk
This is a 15 metre pool in a Grade 2 listed Victorian building. It also provides swimming lessons and is fully operational after a refurbishment. It has aqua natal sessions.

Outdoor Paddling Pools

There are three paddling pools in Brighton & Hove run by the council, Saunders, Hove Lagoon and King's Road. These paddling pools are free and open for the summer season each year, from May until September. There are water play in Yellowave, the Level and rock pooling at Rottingdean. For further information on paddling pools, see the Brighton and Hove Council website: www.brighton-hove.gov.uk/content/leisure-and-libraries/sports-and-activity/paddling-pools

Saunders Park

Lewes Road
www.saunders-park.com
It is near the Vogue Gyratory opposite Lewes Road Bus Garage. It has a play area, paddling pool and community garden. Also basketball/football courts and toilets.

Saltdean Lido - closed until later in 2015

Saltdean, Brighton
http://saltdeanlido.co.uk
This is a fantastic pool. It has a cascade in the centre and a diving board. It has a tea terrace, a sun deck and a café. It is in the Design Museum in London. Designed by Richard Jones. It is leased by the Saltdean Lido Community interest company and plans to reopen in June 2015.

Hove Lagoon

Hove Lagoon, Kingsway, Hove BN3 4LX
A very popular paddling pool. There are public toilets with baby changing facilities close by.

The Level

The Level, Park Crescent, Brighton BN1 4SD
This is a small paddling pool next to a playground and cafe.

King's Road playground

King's Road, Brighton BN1
(by the Old West Pier)

It has a play area and sand pit and gets very busy in the summer months. There are good public toilet facilities and baby change facilities.

Yellowave Beach Sports Centre

Madeira Drive. It's not a paddling pool but has some water play facilities.

Rock Pooling at Rottingdean Beach

Rottingdean Beach – East of Brighton Marina
To the east of Brighton Marina, underneath the white chalk cliffs and rocky beach of Rottingdean. The Volks Railway takes you most of the way there.

Sport Activities

There are many, many sports activities in the local area, from rock climbing to toddler gymnastics, Segways to bowling. Many of these take place in local sports centres, however there is so much more, for example you can play volleyball on the beach for free!

Bowlplex

Marina Way, Brighton BN2 5UT
Tel: 01273 818180
www.bowlplex.co.uk
Ten pin bowling complex. Lane adaptations for kids plus lighter balls.

Preston Park

Preston Road, Brighton
www.brighton-hove.gov.uk/content/leisure-and-libraries/parks-and-green-spaces/preston-park
The largest urban park in the city, four football pitches and two cricket fields, bowling greens, tennis courts, velodrome and more. It also has the oldest and largest Elm trees in the world! Get Bus 5 between Hangleton and Patcham.

Brighton & Hove Albion FC

The American Express Community Stadium, Village Way, East Sussex BN1 9BL
Tel: 0844 3271901
www.seagulls.co.uk.
Nicknamed the 'Seagulls' - Brighton and Hove's football team is based here. The stadium has a dedicated family stand. Tickets from £25 for adults, £10 for under-18s, and £5 for under-10s.

Inaspin: Segways & Zorbing

Tel: 0844 414 8360
www.inaspin.com
In a Spin bring Segways and Zorbing to Brighton Beach, near the old West Pier. Ride in a giant orb or segway.

Yellowave Beach Sports

299 Madeira Drive, Brighton BN2 1EN
Tel: 01273 672222
www.yellowave.co.uk
Beach sports on Brighton's only sandy beach! Barefoot Cafe/Bar with inside and outside areas, a sandy play area for kids, highchairs and baby changing facilities. You can either pay and play by hiring a court with friends, or join an after school or holiday session.

The Brighton Watersports

185 Kings Road Arches, Brighton Seafront, BN1 1NB
Tel: 01273 323160
www.thebrightonwatersports.co.uk
Wake boarding to water skiing. Take a charter boat or hire a kayak. Some of the watersports are only suitable for older children and it is preferable that they can swim.

Sports Centres in Brighton & Hove

Brighton & Hove has a wide range of sport and leisure facilities, from swimming and paddling pools, to sports centres and golf courses. For more information about sports activities in general across the city, see the Brighton & Hove's Active for Life website or call the Sports Development Team on 01273 292724

Hove Lagoon Watersports

Kingsway, Hove BN3 4LX
Tel: 01273 424842
www.hovelagoon.co.uk
Windsurfing and sailing courses for kids (from age 6) with additional activity weeks during the Summer holidays (from age 8). Taught by qualified instructors.

King Alfred Leisure Centre

Kingsway, Hove BN3 2WW
Tel: 01273 290290
www.kingalfredleisure.co.uk
Bus 1, 6, 20, 49 all stop nearby. There are two swimming pools, one of which is reserved for teaching and children's parties. There are two sports halls, for 5-a-side football, badminton, table tennis, volleyball and basketball. There is an outdoor court suitable for tennis. Football courses are offered for children aged 5 - 11 years, and trampolining for those aged 5-12 years. There are mini mayhem soft play sessions for the under 5 yrs on Mondays, Tuesdays and Thursdays from 1:30-2:30pm.

Moulsecoomb Community Leisure Centre

Moulsecoomb Way, Brighton BN2 4PB
moulsecoombenquiries@freedom
leisure.co.uk
Tel: 01273 622266
It has a gym, studio, sports hall and a cafe.

Portslade Sports Centre

Portslade Community College, Chalky Road, Portslade, Brighton BN41 2WS
Tel: 01273 411100
portsladesportscentre.co.uk
Activity classes for children include trampolining, indoor football, Sama karate, gymnastics, badminton, snooker, fencing, Tae Jitsu and basketball.

Stanley Deason Leisure Centre

Wilson Avenue, Brighton BN2 5PB
stanleydeasonenquiries@freedom-leisure.co.uk
Tel: 01273 694281
www.freedom-leisure.co.uk/centres.asp?section=661
 This has a gym, sports hall, 3g artificial pitch, squash courts and a cafe. Trampolining classes on a Saturday plus there is a climbing wall which is run by Adventure Unlimited.

The Deans Leisure Centre

Longhill High School, Falmer Road
Rottingdean, Brighton BN2 7FR
Tel: 01273 391 683
www.deansleisurecentre.co.uk
Studio classes to children's sport academies. The fitness suite includes high quality gym equipment and we offer a wide range of memberships. The centre is located on the grounds of Longhill High School.

Withdean Sports Complex

Tongdean Ln, Brighton
Tel: 01273 542100
www.freedom-leisure.co.uk
Gym, studios, MyRide indoor cycling studio and squash courts. It also has a crèche. Kids can enjoy the climbing wall and there is an athletics track and a cafe.

Golf Courses

Waterhall Golf Course and Hollingbury Park Golf Course, are managed by MyTime Active, monitored by the Sport Facilities Team.

Hollingbury Park Golf Course

Ditchling Road, Brighton BN1 7HS
hollingbury@mytimeactive.co.uk
Tel: 01273 500086
This has lovely views down to the sea. It is an established 18-hole, par 72 layout that in previous years has been a qualifying venue for – The Open. They have lessons for juniors.
Prices
Adult   18 Holes £17.00 -£22.00
Junior   18 Holes £7.00

Rottingdean Miniature Golf and Putting Course

8 Marine Drive, Brighton BN2 7HE
Tel: 01273 302127
An excellent 18 hole pitch and putt which takes approximately one and a half hours to complete. There is a car park nearby and a tea room which is open in the summer.

Waterhall Golf Course

Saddlescombe Road, Brighton BN45 7DB
waterhall@mytimeactive.co.uk
Tel: 01273 508658
An 18-hole course which travels along the Waterhall Valley, with Patcham Windmill overlooking several holes and the Clubhouse. Devil's Dyke is just over the hillside.
Prices
Adult   18 Holes £12.00-£14.00
Junior   18 Holes £7.00

Sports Centres around Sussex

Adur Outdoor Activities Centre

Brighton Road, Shoreham-by-Sea, West Sussex BN43 5LT
Tel: 01273 462928
www.aoac.org.uk

This has a range of outdoor activities. It has a climbing and bouldering wall as well as watersports.

Apollo Lasertag

49 Martlets, Martlet Heights, Burgess Hill, Sussex. RH15 9NN
www.apollolasertag.co.uk
For older children and adults, a fun way to run around playing laser tag. From 7 years upwards.

Bedgebury National Pinetum & Forest

Tel: 01580 879820
www.forestry.gov.uk/bedgebury
Walking, cycling, mountain biking, horse riding and adventure play. A large forest park on the Sussex/Kent border. There are ability trails throughout the Forest and National Pinetum. You can try the 10km family cycle route. There is also a Go Ape high wire forest adventure course with high ropes, bridges and zip wires. The Visitor Centre has a cafe, and a cycle hire shop.

Downs Leisure Centre

Sutton Road, Seaford, East Sussex BN25 4QW
info@waveleisure.co.uk
Tel 01323 490011
www.waveleisure.co.uk
A multi-purpose leisure centre with a gym, sports and activity halls, an outdoor 3G all weather pitch, aerobics studio and café. It also has a soft play area, Dino's. The nearest pool is at Seaford Head.

Fort Fun & Rockys

Royal Parade, Eastbourne, East Sussex BN22 7LQ
Tel: 01323 642833
www.fortfun.co.uk
Indoor and outdoor fun at this adventure park which is home to the first family aqua water park in the South East. Visit Rocky's Adventure Land, the huge indoor play area. It is right on the beach, to the east of the seafront. The aqua splash water park has multiple slides, tilting buckets, interactive play panels, sprinkle showers, snake tunnels & loads more.

Knockhatch Adventure Park

Hailsham Bypass, Hailsham BN27 3PR
info@knockhatch.com
Tel: 01323 442051
www.knockhatch.com
Set in 80 acres of countryside, the park has indoor soft play and outdoor playgrounds. There is a giant leap slide for the adventurous! Also toboggans, trampolines and crazy golf. At extra cost and weather permitting, go-karts, laser adventure game and rodeo bull. There is a kids driving school in electric cars - height limit 0.9m to 1.3m. The boating lake has a waterslide. There is also a paddling pool, and a petting animal farm. New features are the runaway train simulator ride and animal or bird of prey experience.

Knockhatch Adventure Park Ski and Snowboard Centre

Nr Hailsham, BN27 3GD
Tel: 01323 442051
www.knockhatch.com
Knockhatch Adventure Park and the Ski and Snowboard Centre. This has a 110 dry ski slope and nursery slopes. Lessons are available.

Olympos (The Triangle)

The Triangle, Triangle Way, Burgess Hill, Brighton RH15 8WA
Tel: 01444 876001
www.olymposcentres.co.uk
Softplay for the under 8s. It has a 25m indoor pool, outdoor pool, flumes, watersprays, waterfalls and rapids.

Peacehaven Leisure Centre

Greenwich Way, Peacehaven, East Sussex BN10 8BB
info@waveleisure.co.uk
Tel: 01273 588858
www.waveleisure.co.uk
This has a gym, sports halls, squash courts, the Magic Castle soft play

centre. It is located next to the Meridian Shopping Centre.

Qleisure Ltd

London Road, Albourne, West Sussex, BN6 9BQ
Tel: 01273 834403
www.qleisure.co.uk
Qleisure Ltd Activity centre for older kids offering go karting (and a Kids Karting club), quad biking, archery and clay pigeon. For kids of 8 years and older.

Ringmer Swimming Pool

Lewes Road, Ringmer, East Sussex BN8 5RB
info@waveleisure.co.uk
Tel: 01273 813533
www.waveleisure.co.uk
The pool has lane swimming, water aerobics classes and swimming lessons.

Seahaven Swim & Fitness Centre

Chapel Street, Newhaven, East Sussex BN9 9PN
info@waveleisure.co.uk
Tel: 01273 512498
www.waveleisure.co.uk
Located in central Newhaven, this has a 25m pool, a toddler pool, exercise classes and gym.

Seaford Head Pool

Sutton Avenue, Seaford, East Sussex BN25 4LX
Tel 01323 897632
www.waveleisure.co.uk
Seaford Head Pool has lane swimming, water aerobics classes and swimming lessons.

Seaford Head Sports Facility

Steyne Road, Seaford, East Sussex, BN25 1AL
Tel: 01323 490011
www.waveleisure.co.uk
Just 10 minutes from the Downs Leisure Centre. It has a sports hall, dance studio and climbing wall.

Southwick Leisure Centre

Impulse Leisure, Old Barn Way, BN42 4NT
Tel: 01273 238111
www.impulseleisure.co.uk/Southwick
Provides a range of activities for kids from toddlers to teens. Roller hockey, football, badminton and trampolining for 5 -16 year olds. Dance classes for 6 - 16 years and several different toddler sessions.

TeamSport Go Karting Brighton

30 Chartwell Rd, Lancing Business Park, Lancing, West Sussex
Tel: 844 998 0000
www.team-sport.co.uk/brighton
For kids of 8 years and older. A day out racing around the track for the speedy kids.

The Pells Outdoor Swimming Pool

Brook Street, Lewes, BN7 2BA
thepellspool@yahoo.co.uk
Tel: 01273 472334
www.pellspool.org.uk
The outdoor pool in Lewes is the oldest and one of the largest freshwater pools in the country. It also has children's paddling pool, sunbathing terrace and a cafe. The terrace is on a tree lined lawn, perfect for summer days. It is open from May to September. Recent excavations show that the present pool tank, lies within two previous shells.

Waterlea Adventure Park

Furnace Green, Crawley (near the Hawth Centre)
Tel: 01293 530035
www.crawley.gov.uk/stellent/idcplg?IdcService=SS_GET_PAGE&ssDocName=INT010139
This council run adventure playground offers a large outdoor adventure play area with an underwater theme with rope walls, ladders and slides, a more conventional play area and an indoor play hall. Refreshments are available. There is also a shop and picnic areas. Check opening times as they vary.

Worthing Leisure Centre

Shaftesbury Avenue, Durrington, BN12 4ET
Tel: 01903 502237
www.worthingleisure.co.uk
Football, badminton, basketball, gymnastics, trampolining, plus activities for toddlers.

ARTS & MUSIC
GALLERIES & COURSES

It can be good to get a child's perspective on art in a gallery. You may be surprised at what they may like! There are arts and music everywhere; at the many festivals and events; at toddler music groups and sculpture trails.

You may have a child who is keen on ballet or hip hop, a budding chef, guitar player or Picasso. You can nurture their creative appetites with some of the local classes on offer. These are advertised on local websites and in music schools. Some of these are listed here however there are many more.

Brighton is known as a media centre, with many musicians, poets and artists having made it their home through the years. Who knows, one day maybe your child will become one of them!

Galleries & Sculpture in Sussex

Pallant House Gallery
9 North Pallant, Chichester, West Sussex PO19 1TJ
Tel: 01243 774557
www.pallant.org.uk
Housed in a Grade 1 listed town house, a collection of 20th century and contemporary art. It all started with the personal collection of Walter Hussey, the dean of Chichester Cathedral. Includes art work by Henry Moore and Charles Kearley. Closed Mondays.

Cass Sculpture Foundation
New Barn Hill, Goodwood, Chichester PO18 0QP
Tel: 01243 538449
www.sculpture.org.uk
This is a charitable foundation established in 1992 by Wilfred and Jeannette Cass. There are 26 acres grounds which have an ever-changing display of 80 monumental sculptures. See the 'Dreamy Bathroom' by Gary Webb or Eva Rathschild web like building. The 'Exotic tree' by Zadoc Ben-David is lovely. It is closed for winter. Admission: £10 per person, children under 12, £5, under 5's free.

Towner Art Gallery
Devonshire Park, College Road, Eastbourne BN21 4JJ
towner@eastbourne.gov.uk
Tel: 01323 434670
www.townereastbourne.org.uk
Minimalism and modernism in architecture and art. It is an interesting place both inside and out. Closed Mondays.

Arts & Drama Courses

Active Kids Theatre
Tel: 01273 818266

70

www.actbrighton.org
Classes in drama for children and young people.

Brighton Theatre Group

btg.keepingintouch@hotmail.co.uk
www.brightontg.com
Established since 1968. They perform across Sussex and at Brighton's famous Theatre Royal. The subsidiary company BTG Youth is a popular youth production company giving musical theatre experience to those aged between 9 - 18 years.

City Youth Theatre Company

www.cityyouththeatre.co.uk
The City Youth Theatre Company runs theatre arts related workshops, for children and young people aged 8 years and over.

Get Creative in Patcham

Tel: 07967 633438
Drama, dance, circus, art and craft workshops for children aged 18 months - 11 years. Drama Tots: A gentle and fun sessions for 18 months - 4 year olds, full of story-telling, puppets and dressing up.

Hangleton Brass and Youth Band

Tel: 01273 388702
www.hangletonband.co.uk
Hangleton Brass Band are the only brass band in the area with charitable status.

Italia Conti Performing Arts Associates

Tel: 01273 321245
www.italiaconticlaphamandbrighton.co.uk
Classes include: musical theatre, singing, street/jazz dance, acting exams, ballet, tap, contemporary and hip-hop.

Kids@Komedia

Tel: 0845 293 8480
www.komedia.co.uk

Voted Best Family Friendly Theatre in The South. Kids@Komedia shows are a huge hit with kids and their families alike.

Shana Goldman's Stage School & Agency

Tel: 01323 472391
www.shanagoldmans.co.uk
Goldmans Stage School runs weekly classes in Ballet, Jazz, Tap, Singing & Acting for children aged 3 upwards. All of the teachers are professional performers.

Stagecoach Theatre Arts (Hove)

Tel: 01273 258318
www.stagecoach.co.uk
Part-time tuition in dance, drama and singing for children aged 4-18 years.

The Circus Project

Tel: 01273 739106
www.thecircusproject.co.uk
A registered charity launched in 2000, Classes and workshops specialising in aerial circus (trapeze, rope and silks).

Workshops for the Imagination

Tel: 07939 482 361
www.workshopsfortheimagination.com
An art studio for children. Art, music and creative play for 2-3 year olds.

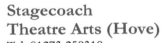

Dance

Brighton & Hove Music & Arts

County Oak Avenue, Brighton BN1 8DJ
bhma@brighton-hove.gov.uk

Tel: 01273 293524
www.bhma.org.uk

Young Dancers Collective

38-42 Brunswick St West Hove East Sussex BN3 1EL
An open access weekly dance class for 13 to 17 year olds.

Youth Dance Company

This exciting group changes from project to project and is open to students aged between 16 and 19 years.
For both projects:
Tel: 01273 293621
laura.woods@brighton-hove.gov.uk
www.bhma.org.uk

Alexandra Dance Academy

Tel: 01273 565881
www.alexandradance.co.uk
Ballet, modern, street dance, and tap, starting from pre-school beginners through to advanced major grades.

Beacon Arts

Tel: 01273 557124
www.beaconarts.co.uk

Ballet, drama and music classes for children.

Dance Art Studio

Tel: 01273 556313
www.danceartstudio.co.uk
Dance, drama and singing. The Pre School ballet classes are suitable for 3 – 5 year olds.

Hove Dance Centre

Tel: 01273 419900
www.hovedancecentre.co.uk
Disco, Street, Ballroom and Latin American dancing for children aged from 4 to 16 years old.

Rox School of Dance and Drama

sophierox@btconnect.com
Tel: 01273 208513
www.roxschoolofdancing.co.uk
From ages 2.5 years to adults, dance, drama, singing and yoga.

South East Dance

www.southeastdance.org.uk
Supports those who work in dance and encourages more people to participate in dance.

Tatty Bumpkin

Tel: 08456 808041
www.tattybumpkin.com
Yoga inspired multi-sensory music and movement class for children aged from 2 years to 7 years old.

Music

Brighton & Hove has a thriving live music scene. Many are small venues dotted around the centre and on the seafront. It also has an award winning Music & Arts Service. Other notable music organisations include Brighton Live; The Great Escape Festival and Brighton Institute of Modern Music.

Brighton & Hove Music & Arts

County Oak Avenue,
Brighton BN1 8DJ
bhma@brighton-hove.gov.uk
Tel: 01273 293524

What age should my child start more formal music lessons?

There is no set age for lessons to start, and different teaching methods advise different ages. A good time is when a child is able to concentrate for longer periods, and shows an interest in playing an instrument. As a rough guide, 5-6 years earliest for piano and violin, 7 for guitar, 8/9 years for drums and wind instruments.

Music and a Child's Brain

Musicians have been shown to have significantly more developed left planum temporales, and have also shown to have a greater word memory. Musicians have larger brain volumes in brain areas which may cross over to speech areas.

Journal Nature Reviews Neuroscience 11, 599-605 (2010)

McMaster University have discovered that one-year-old babies who participate in interactive music classes with their parents smile more, communicate better and show earlier and more sophisticated brain responses to music.

Gerry et al (2012) Development Science; Vol 15, Issue 3; p398-407 May
http://en.wikipedia.org/wiki/Cognitive_neuroscience_of_music

www.bhma.org.uk
Provides high quality music and performance opportunities for all children and young people across the city. Music and arts courses for children from year 2 to year 9. There are 'Open Access' courses which require no previous experience as well are more experienced musicians. This including music lessons, workshops, orchestras, summer schools and dance classes. Course fees begin from £30 for 1-day courses. A Subsidised Course Scheme is available for children and young people from families on low incomes. They are the lead partner of the award winning SoundCity, the Music Education Hub for Brighton & Hove.

SoundCity

Tel: 01273 293524
www.soundcitybh.org
SoundCity, the Brighton & Hove Music Education Hub, brings together the leading organisations for music in the city.

British and Irish Modern Music Institute

http://www.bimm.co.uk
Provider of contemporary music education in London, Brighton, Manchester, Bristol and Dublin. Offers Higher and Further Education music courses – including BA Honours Degrees. Includes guitar, bass, drums, vocals, songwriting, music production, music business and event management.

Public Art

There are many artworks all around Brighton and Hove, in the street furnitiure, lighting, buildings and sculptures. See how many you can find!

Public art trails

These trails invite you to explore public artworks by Brighton and Hove City Council. They include a dark walk to see the illuminated work, a seafront trail and Hove trail. See their website for details: www.journeyon.co.uk.

Brighton Seafront Art Trail

You can see many art installations on this bright and breezy walk around the seafront. You can take in the 'Twins', the 'Black Lion Street Railings' and the famous 'Kiss Wall'.

1. Start at Brighton Station. Head towards the sea along Queen's Road.
2. By the Clocktower find **'Write Around Air Street'** - poems on the theme of air which is on the street furniture near here.
3. Go along Air Street, and cross the road at Queen Square and continue on down Western Road onto Churchill Square. Here you'll see the 'Twins'.
4. Walk back along Western road and into West Street, the major street to the seafront. Cross the road at the traffic lights, walk down and see **'Avalon Gate'**, a huge metal gate at the entrance to the Avalon development.

5. You should also be able to see three brighly coloured light sculptures at the bottom of West St. These are **'The Cones'**.
6. Cross over onto the seafront promenade. See **'Passacaglia'**, a large recycled iron sculpture right on the beach. You will also find the 'Kiss Wall' near here.
7. Turn away from the Pier onto a groyne where there is a big circular, bronze sculpture, 'Afloat'.
8. Head back towards the town, and right after the Thistle Hotel on to Black Lion Street. Find the blue sculptural **'Black Lion Street Railings'**.
9. Head back into town now. Walk along Prince Albert Street, in to the famous shopping Lanes along Meeting House Lane. Continue until you get to North Street. Cross at the traffic lights and turn right until you get to New Road where you will find **'Drift'**.
10. Continue along New Road, cross straight over Church Street and on to Jubilee Street to the Library. Here are the artworks **'Under-Discover'**, **'Liquidus'** and **'The Wall of A Thousand Stories'**.
11. Continue to North Road and wind your way north to Kensington Street, the pedestrianised busy shopping street. You are now in the North Laines. Continue up the main shopping streets until you get to Trafalgar Street.
12. Continue over the road to Whitecross Street. You will get to New England Street, Cheapside and the **New England Quarter Artworks.**
13. **The Urban Art Wall** runs along New England Quarter.

Art Galleries in Brighton

AM Gallery
1 Borough Street, Brighton
Tel: 01273 771228

Art at five
5 Bartholomews, Brighton BN1 1HG
Tel: 01273 774222

Artique Gallery
44 Market Street, Brighton BN1 1HH
Tel: 01273 710660

ArtRepublic
13 Bond Street, Brighton
Tel: 0845 644 5334

Blank Studios
108 North St, Portslade, Brighton BN41 1DG
Tel: 07946 465942

Brighton Media Centre Gallery
15-17 Middle Street, Brighton BN1 1AL
Tel: 01273 201100

Brighton Museum & Art Gallery
Royal Pavilion Gardens, Brighton
Tel: 03000 290900

Crane Kalman Brighton
38 Kensington Gardens, Brighton
Tel: 01273 697096

Daniel Laurence Home and Garden
226 Kings Road Arches, Brighton BN1 1NB
Tel: 01273 739694

Hove Museum & Art Gallery
19 New Church Road, Hove
Tel: 03000 290900

Ink-d
96 North Rd, Brighton
Tel: 01273 645299

iO Gallery
39 Sydney Street, Brighton BN1 4EP
Tel: 01273 671212

Linda Boucher
234 Kings Road Arches, Brighton BN1 1NB

Tel: 01273 779937

One Eyed Jacks Gallery
28 York Pl, Brighton BN4 1GU
Tel: 07743 098530

Open Gallery
Unit 1, 29-42 Windsor Street, Brighton
Tel: 01273 325041

Fabrica
Holy Trinity Church, Ship Street, Brighton
Tel: 01273 778646

First Light Photographic Gallery
3 Nile Street, Brighton BN1 1HN
Tel: 01273 327344

Gallery 100
100 Queen's Road, Brighton
Tel: 01273 744205

George Street Gallery
4 George Street, Brighton
Tel: 01273 681852

Naked Eye
5 Farm Mews, Farm Road, Hove BN3 1GH
Tel: 01273 204800

North Laine Photography Gallery
7-8 Kensington Gardens, Brighton BN1 4AL
Tel: 01273 628794

Phoenix Brighton
10–14 Waterloo Place, Brighton BN2 9NB
Tel: 01273 603700

Permanent Gallery
20 Bedford Place, Brighton
Tel: 01273 710771

The Rodhus Gallery
16-30 Hollingdean Road, Brighton BN2 4AA
Tel: 01273 694124

Seafront Image
Brighton Fishing Museum, 202 Kings Road Arches, Brighton BN1 1NB
Tel: 01273 725777

Two Kats and a Cow Gallery
167 Kings Road Arches,Brighton Beach BN1 1NB
Tel: 01273 776746

J'Adore Art
2 Nile Pavilions Nile Street Brighton BN1 1HW
Tel: 01273 776070

University of Brighton Gallery
Grand Parade, Brighton
Tel: 01273 643010

10 Things to do Outside Before you are 10

1. Play 'Pooh' sticks, like Pooh Bear, race sticks from a bridge.

2. Roll down a hill. A small one. One where you can stop on grass and not a road!

3. Find a minibeast with a magnifying glass and find out what it is.

4. Skim a stone across a lake.

5. Splash about in the rain, in a puddle, in wellington boots.

Growing potatoes

6. Fly a kite. The Downs have some good hills to try flying your kite.

7. Go sledging and/or build a snowman in the snow.

8. Learn to ride a bike.

9. Kick around in autumn leaves. Find chestnuts and play conkers. See the squirrels scamper around.

10. Plant something, grow it, eat it! (Make sure it's edible!)

EVENTS CALENDAR

There are some wonderful, quirky and inspiring events around Brighton and Sussex. The summer gets busy with the Brighton Festival and it's equally fun packed fringe. The Children's parade has a different theme every year.

January

Robbie Burns Night - 25th
Various, Sussex
Eat Haggis on Burns night, various restaurants and pubs around Sussex.

February

Brighton Science Festival
www.brightonscience.com
Fun scientific events many aimed at young teenagers. In 2014 they had raspberry pi workshops (computer programming), Lego robotics, paper magic tricks and more.

March

SICK! Festival
www.sickfestival.com
This new festival explores the physical, mental and social challenges of life and death.

The Chocolate Festival
www.festivalchocolate.co.uk
Handy for Easter, indulge your sweet tooth at this chocolate event.

WhaleFest
www.whale-fest.com
A family friendly event about whales and dolphins and the marine environment.

VegFestUK
ww.vegfest.co.uk
Over 100 stalls and competitions on the best of vegetarian food. With films, cooking demonstrations, music, and talks.

April

Brighton & Hove Food and Drink Festival
www.festivalchocolate.co.uk/festivals/
Celebrates local producers, growers, restaurants, bars and food retailers.Victoria Gardens. Two days of food fun.

Brighton Marathon
www.brightonmarathon.co.uk
This is now one of the big marathons (the top 12) in the UK.

Eastbourne Festival

www.eastbournefestival.co.uk
Music, arts and comedy with an annual 'shout singing' event on the beach.

May

Brighton Festival

www.brightonfestival.org
This is the biggest arts festival in the UK. It has a fantastic array of art and entertainment. Founded in 1966, it is the biggest multi-artform festival in England. The events vary each year but promise a huge amount of music, Shakespeare, dance and more.

Brighton Fringe

www.brightonfestivalfringe.org.uk, early-late May
This is the third largest Fringe Festival in the world. There are a myriad of events, from street performances to comedy, music, clubs, theatre and exhibitions.

Brighton Children's Parade

www.samesky.co.uk/events/childrens-parade
Thousands of children from schools and community groups across the region take to Brighton's streets dressed in costumes they have designed and made for this annual parade.

Artists Open Houses

www.aoh.org.uk
A nice way to see local art and meet the artists, by being displayed in peoples' houses. It is also affordable way to buy art.

Charleston Festival

www.charleston.org.uk/what's-on/festivals/the-Charleston-festival/
Talks, discussions, films and workshops inspired by the Bloomsbury Group of writers, painters and intellectuals.

Elderflower Festival

www.elderflowerfields.co.uk
A small 'boutique' festival in the Sussex countryside.

Foodies Festival

http://foodiesfestival.com/event/brighton-hove-lawns/
Takes place in Hove Lawns to enjoy an array of culinary activities including a live entertainment stage, cooking demonstrations and tasty treats from some of the city's top restaurants.

Jack in the Green Festival - hastings

www.visit1066country.com/events
Troupes of morris dancers and giants parade through the streets to welcome in the summer.

The Great Escape

http://greatescapefestival.com
A music festival, with over 200 new local and international artists across 35 venues over 3 days.

Tulip Festival

www.pashleymanorgardens.com
Pashley Manor Gardens
An array of lovely tulips, thousands of them.

June

Brighton's Big Screen on the Beach

A big screen on the seafront with movies and sports to liven up the summer days.

Glyndebourne Opera House

http://glyndebourne.com/
Set near Lewes, this famous festival in the beautiful grounds of the Glyndebourne Opera House has been attracting people for many years. Take a posh picnic and listen to the sound of tenors and baritones.

Sussex Festival of Nature

www.brighton-hove.gov.uk/content/leisure-and-libraries/Sussex-festival-nature
A celebration of local wildlife and wildlife-friendly living. Great little festival in Stanmer Park. See birds of prey, sheep shearing, heavy horses.

July

Brighton Kite Festival

www.brightonkiteflyers.co.uk/festival/
Stunning aerial displays of kites in Stanmer Park.

Love Supreme Festival

www.lovesupremefestival.com
Jazz artists at this new festival in Glynde, near Lewes. Accessible by shuttle bus from Brighton.

Paddle Round the Pier

www.paddleroundthepier.com
This is Europe's largest annual beach festival takes place by Hove Lawns and on the beachfront. Lots of events for novices and serious athletes, and of course the Paddle Around the Pier!

The Awesome Shoreham Chilli Festival

www.visitworthing.co.uk/what's-on/the-4th-awesome-shoreham-chilli-festival-p103164
If you love chilli then you'll love this, with chilli's in pickles, in chocolate, in cheese…

Worthing Lions Festival

www.worthinglions.co.uk
Family fun including fireworks and a bus rally.

August

Arundel Festival

www.arundelfestival.co.uk
It's worth going just to see the bathtub race! There are street entertainers and a gallery trail.

Brighton Pride
www.brighton-pride.org
Brighton Pride celebrates everything lesbian, gay, bisexual and transgender. It is family friendly and has stalls, music and entertainment at the parades end, Preston Park.

Brighton MOD Weekender
The original celebration of sixties modernist style. See the Vespas bikes descend on Brighton seafront. Usually August bank holiday.

Brunswick Festival
http://brunswickfestival.org.uk
A friendly neighbourhood festival in the Brunswick area of Hove, with street theatre and jazz.

Brighton Racecourse August Festival
www.brighton-racecourse.co.uk
Dress up and see the horse racing in the course high up above Brighton.

Medieval Festival at Herstmonceux Castle
www.englandsmedievalfestival.com
A big celebration of the middle ages, held at the castle.

Tribal Earth Festival
www.tribalearth.co.uk
A small four day festival in Laughton, near Lewes workshops, music, camping & community spirit.

September

Artwave Festival in Lewes
www.artwavefestival.org
Arts and crafts in the Lewes area.

Brighton Food & Drink Festival
http://brightonfoodfestival.com/
It is the largest food festival in the south of England, running in Easter and September for 10 days.

Brighton Japan Festival
www.brightonjapan.com
A celebration of Japanese theatre, performance, arts, films and culture.

Brighton Art Fair
www.brightonartfair.co.uk
A huge exhibition of painters, printmakers, photographers and sculptors.

Brighton Digital Festival

www.brightondigitalfestival.co.uk
A season of exhibitions, performances, meet-ups, workshops and outdoor events.

Shoreham Airshow

A great family day out especially if your kids like planes.

City Reads

http://cityreads.co.uk
Aims to spread a love of books and ideas to the city.

Slindon Estate

Top Road, Slindon, near Arundel, West Sussex, BN18 0RG
Tel: 01243 814730
www.nationaltrust.org.uk/slindon-estate
Autumn brings Slindon's famous pumpkin display, and a fantastic leafy show of colours in Park Wood.

October

Brighton Photo Biennial

http://bpb.org.uk/2014/
International photographic practice celebration.

Brighton Comedy Festival

www.brightoncomedyfestival.com
3 weeks of comedy, from new and established comics.

Brighton Early Music Festival

www.bremf.org.uk
A celebration of early music.

Brighton Fashion Week

www.brightonfashionweek.com
If you'd like to see local up-and-coming designers then this is the event. With a catwalk show, great parties and a fashion emporium.

Apple Festival at Middle Farm

www.middlefarm.com/whats-on/
A celebration of apples in this pretty part of the South Downs.

November

London to Brighton Veteran Car Run

www.veterancarrun.com
See some wonderful vintage cars. The world's longest running motoring event. It is featured in the film Genevieve.

CINECITY

www.cine-city.co.uk

A global mix of premieres and previews, treasures from the archives plus the latest digital adventures.

Colour Out of Space

www.colouroutofspace.org
A festival of experimental music and film.

Lewes Bonfire Night

www.lewesbonfirecelebrations.com
The biggest bonfire night in the UK with torch lit processions, fireworks. Gets very busy particularly if you have young kids.

December

Burning the Clocks

www.samesky.co.uk/events/burning-the-clocks
The parade of lanterns through Brighton, culminating in a firework display. Takes place every year on the Winter Solstice (21st December).

Make your own Dragon Cake

PARTY IDEAS

1. **Adventure Unlimited Birthday Parties** - Indoor Rock Climbing or archery.
www.aultd.org/climbing-wall/birthday-parties

2. **Big Bead Boutique** – Make your own jewellery, leave with a personalised bracelet.
www.bigbeadboutique.co.uk

3. **Blackberry farm** - use the play areas, see the animals and for an extra charge, tractor rides.
www.blackberry-farm.co.uk

4. **Brighton & Hove Climbing Centre** -Another climbing adventure centre. *www.high-sports.co.uk*

5. **Tutu Tales** Ballet and music for children aged 2.5 to 7 years, incorporating story-telling and props.
www.tututales.co.uk

6. **Lazer Tag at Funplex** Battle weapon parties or indoor soft play. *www.funplex.co.uk*

7. **Pizza Express** – Make Your Own Pizza Party – with a balloon and certificate to take home.
www.pizzaexpress.com/parties/kidspizzamaking

8. **Bandbazi Children's Circus parties**– Juggling, plate spinning, poi, static trapeze, acrobalance and rope performances, kids invited to join or assist. www.bandbazi.co.uk

9. **Popstar Party** – Record their own songs at Zanosound recording studios. *www.zanosound.com*

10. **Baby Sensory**– Birthday parties for 1-3 year olds, light shows, music, glowing bouncy balls, bubbles, bells and songs. *www.cambridgekungfu.com/kids/parties*

Do It Yourself
Alternatively, you can organise your own party, with finger food, treats, fun and games, at your home or outside as a picnic. Smaller children could play traditional games like musical chairs or 'Simon says', and you can rope in help from other parents. Some people hire a local hall or a bouncy castle. Party bags, if you want them, can work out expensive. Instead you could buy a set of books like the Mr Men series or do a lucky dip, or get the kids to decorate their own cup cake to take away.

PLACES TO STAY

Places to Stay

Check the Tourist Information Centres for local cottages and hotels. There are many to choose from. Here are a few family favourites that should meet different accommodation needs. From budget camping or youth hostelling, to modern hotels and apartments.

Brighton Hotels

Artist Residence
33 Regency Square Brighton BN1 2GG
This hotel has individually styled rooms, such as 'Medium Arty Sea View'; 'Small House'; 'Bigger House Sea-View'. It is near the beach and Churchill Square Shopping Centre.

Blanch House
17 Atlingworth Street, Brighton BN21PL
This is in the more expensive end, however this grade II listed building has only 12 en-suite rooms that are cosy and welcoming. It has an award-winning 70's lounge-chic cocktail bar, and a good in-house restaurant. Each room is individually themed with reylon beds, fogarty goose and duck down duvets and pillows. You may want to stay here with the kids at their grandparents...

Jurys Inn Brighton
101 Stroudley Road, Brighton
Right next to the railway station Jurys Inn Brighton is in the heart of the New England quarter. It has moderately priced family accommodation and near all the attractions.

Myhotel
17 Jubilee Street, Brighton, East-Sussex
This new (2008) 80-guestroom hotel, the inspiration of Andy Thrasyvoulou and New York designer Karim Rashid. It is in the heart of the North Laines, 10 minutes from the seafront. It's décor is clean and modern.

Seattle Hotel
Brighton Marina Brighton BN2 5WA
This is further out of town, in the Marina, but right by the sea. It is modern and clean.

Camping and Caravanning
Brakes Coppice Park
Crowhurst, Battle, East Sussex TN33 9AB
Tel: 01424 830322
brakesco@btinternet.com
www.brakescoppicepark.co.uk
Open: 1 March-31 October

Chestnut Meadow Camping & Caravan Park
Ninfield Road, Bexhill-on-Sea, East Sussex TN39 5JG
Tel: 01424 892361
info@chestnutmeadow.co.uk
www.chestnutmeadow.co.uk
Open: 1 April-October

Cobbs Hill Farm Caravan & Camping Park

Watermill Lane, Bexhill-on-Sea, East Sussex TN39 5JA
Tel: 01424 213460
cobbshillfarmuk@hotmail.com
www.cobbshillfarm.co.uk
Open: April-October

Kloofs Caravan Park
Sandhurst Lane, Whydown, Bexhill-on-Sea, East Sussex TN39 4RG
Tel: 01424 842839
camping@kloofs.com
www.kloofs.com
Open: All year

Peel House Farm Caravan Park
Sayerland Lane, Polegate, East Sussex BN26 6QX
Tel: 01323 845629
peelhousefarmcp@btinternet.com
www.peelhousefarm.com
Open: April-October

Fairfields Farm Caravan & Camping Park
Westham, Eastbourne Road, Pevensey, East Sussex BN24 5NG
Tel: 01323 763165
enquiries@fairfieldsfarm.com
www.fairfieldsfarm.com
Open: April-October

Norman's Bay Camping and Caravanning Club Site
Normans Bay, Pevensey, East Sussex BN24 6PR
Tel: 01323 761190
www.campingandcaravanningclub.co.uk
Open: April-October

Heaven Farm
Furner's Green, Uckfield, East Sussex TN22 3RG
Tel: 01825 790226
heavenfarmleisure@btinternet.com
www.heavenfarm.co.uk
Open: Touring caravans all year
Tents: May-October

White Horse Caravan Park
Paddock Lane, Selsey, West Sussex PO20 9EJ
Tel: 01243 606080
holidays@bunnleisure.co.uk
www.bunnleisure.co.uk

Open: March-October

Campervans
Yet another option is to hire a motorhome or campervan. It's more expensive than hiring a car but it does help you save on accommodation costs, and gives almost unlimited freedom. Internet sites to check include these:
Cool Campervans - www.coolcampervans.com
Just Go - www.justgo.uk.com
Wild Horizon - www.wildhorizon.co.uk

East Sussex Hotels
Ashdown Park Hotel
Forest Row
Tel: 01342 824 988
A relatively new hotel, with extensive grounds. It runs tasty gourmet evenings every year, including a chocoholic one. From £135pp a night B&B.

The Big Sleep Hotel
King Edwards Parade, Eastbourne, BN21 4EB
Right on Eastbourne's seafront, this has reasonable modern accommodation just 400 metres from Eastbourne town centre. Some rooms feature sea views. They have pool, darts, and table tennis facilities available in the games room.

Jeake's House Hotel
Mermaid Street, Rye, East Sussex TN31 7ET
This has quirky interiors and is a Tuscany trattoria feel. The beds are traditional, quilted or lace, antique furniture. Breakfast is served in the galleried former chapel, where you can choose from devilled kidneys, Rye Rarebit and boiled eggs and Marmite soldiers. There is also an honesty bar and a quiet parlour.

Self Catering
Fox Hall
West Sussex
landmarktrust.org.uk
Built in 1730 in the elegant Palladian style. It was once a meeting place for

the 18th century's fashionable set. The main bed is in a gilded alcove, however there's also a plainer twin-bedroom. It sleeps four, from £339 for four nights;

Laguna Beach House
Camber, East Sussex
Tel: 01242 522525
camberbeachhouses.co.uk
It has three funky bedrooms and a big south-facing roof terrace with sunloungers, hammocks and barbecue. It is right next to the sandy beach with grassy dunes, this retreat has Sleeps eight, from £1,500 a week

Pelham House
St Andrews Lane, Lewes BN7 1UW
A beautiful 16th century listed townhouse, 5-minutes walk from Lewes Rail Station.

South Downs YHA
Itford Farm, Beddingham, Lewes
A refurbished Sussex farmhouse and barn buildings right on the South Downs Way. You can get there from a short walk down a country lane from Southease Railway station. It has extensive grounds, which the family can explore to see local wildlife or just relax and unwind.

The Oast House
Shoreham, Kent
Tel: 01386 701177; ruralretreats.co.uk
Beautiful accommodation. It has a woodburning fire and spiral steps up to a bedroom and a private walled garden. Guests can use the owner's swimming pool and tennis court. From £584 a week

Withyfield Cottage
Bines Green, West Sussex
our-land.co.uk
An eco haven. This has been made by local craftsmen using locally grown oak, cedar, pine, sealed with clay and insulated with straw. Sleeps two to six, from £640 a week.

LONDON
DAY OUT

Kings Cross Train Station

Getting There (from Cambridge)

Car - 2 hours 5 minutes (central London) via the M23 and A23.

Train - 1 hour 15 minutes (to London Bridge, London St Pancras International and London Victoria. Watch the times that you can travel, often commuter times can be much more expensive and crowded. A family rail ticket or network card can cut the costs. Although a super off peak day return can be as little as £10 to £15. A family and friends railcard can be handy. The card costs £30 for one year and it gives a third off adult fares and 60% off kids fares.

Bus National Express number 025 from Pool Valley Coach Station (Pool Valley, Brighton near the Pier) - 2 hours 30 minutes to London Victoria

Getting Around

It does get crowded in London, so it is wise to keep an extra eye on children, particularly in getting on and off buses and tubes, and try to avoid rush hour. However, it now much easier with buggies and baby changing with better facilities on public transport and better accessibility. All London taxis are also wheelchair accessible. The main website with details of buses and tubes is Transport for London. www.tfl.gov.uk

Bus

All of the 700 London buses are able to take buggies, and have low floors, but can get crowded at tourist areas and at commuter times. A person with a buggy can use the wheelchair space if someone is not using is, but if a wheelchair gets on they have priority.

Barclays Cycle Hire

www.tfl.gov.uk/road users/cycling
They have a distinct blue mud guard. You can pick up a bike from several docking terminals, paying with your credit or debit card. And then when you've finished, you just dock it back.

The website has cycling safety tips for around London.

By Boat

The Thames has many river cruises, for example from Tate Britain to Tate Modern which only takes 20 minutes, or a longer trip to Greenwich.

London Taxis

The Black London Hackney Cabs can be hailed by the road or at taxi ranks. Fares are displayed.

London Underground

Free for accompanied children under 11. Some tube stations now have lifts and disability access, so if you have a buggy, a disability and/or several kids this can be handy. A full list of these stations are available on the website 'step free' or phone to order the guide on 0343 222 1234. There is also a tube toilet map. Use the wider gates at the ticket barriers.
www.tfl.gov.uk/gettingaround

Oyster Cards

You can purchase these at most London Underground stations, and they can be very handy otherwise you will have to rely on ticket machines for each journey. Or you could get a London day travel card with travel in London included.

Kid Friendly Attractions

Some of the best things to do with children in London are free; the Science Museum, Tate Galleries; walking down the Southbank and seeing the different buskers, performers and skateboarders.

In the summer the beautiful parks in London come alive with people. Hyde Park, Regents Park and St James Park are well maintained and great for picnics, to play games or wander around. Hampstead Heath and Richmond Park are huge and also great to explore. There are playparks dotted around the city, and Corams Fields are central. Further afield, there are Theme Parks. There is a lot of choice for eating out, and although it can be expensive, there are many budget and interesting family friendly places.

Museums

British Museum

Great Russell St, London WC1B 3DG
Nearest tube station: Tottenham Court Rd/Holborn
The Egyptian mummies and huge ancient Roman and Greek sculptures are favourites with kids. The huge, airy main hall is wonderful.

Horniman Museum

100 London Rd, London SE23 3PQ
www.horniman.ac.uk
Nearest train station: Forest Hill Train Station
16 acres of landscaped gardens, a family friendly anthropological museum with many hands on activities. It's a bit out of the centre though.

London Transport Museum

Covent Garden Piazza, London WC2E 7BB
www.ltmuseum.co.uk
Nearest tube station: Covent Garden
Great for any child that likes buses and trains. You can guide a tube through tunnels on a simulator.

Natural History Museum - Free

Cromwell Rd, London SW7 5BD
www.nhm.ac.uk
Nearest tube station: South Kensington
The huge dinosaur skeleton is a great way to introduce children to the wonders of the ancient natural world. But there is much more, such as the earthquake simulator and life size blue whale.

V&A Museum of Childhood - Free

Cambridge Heath Rd, London E2 9PA
www.museumofchildhood.org.uk
Nearest tube station: Bethnal Green (no lift)
Many toys behind glass but also ones that you can touch and play with in 'activity stations', with lego, sandpit etc.

Tate Modern & Tate Britain - Free

Tate Modern, Bankside, London SE1 9TG
Nearest tube station: Southwark
Tate Britain, Millbank, London SW1P 4RG
Nearest tube station: Pimlico
www.tate.org.uk
Both of these can be fantastic places to bring kids, with huge rooms filled with modern and historic art.

National Army Museum - Free

Royal Hospital Rd, London SW3 4HT
www.nam.ac.uk
Nearest tube station: Sloane Square
This has a great kid's zone for under 10's, they can dress up in soldier's uniforms, rock climb, crawl through tunnels. The Kids Zone has a small charge.

Science Museum - Free

Exhibition Rd, London SW7 2DD
www.sciencemuseum.org.uk
Nearest tube station: South Kensington
An amazing place to stimulate your child's curiosity. It has new exhibitions on the Hadron Collider, exploring the Universe, and loads of interactive exhibits, This has a garden for 3-6 year olds with a multi-sensory area and giant building blocks.

HMS Belfast

The Queen's Walk, Tooley Street SE1 2JH
www.iwm.org.uk/visits/hms-belfast
Nearest tube station: London Bridge
Europe's largest preserved World War II warship, great for exploring and imagining what life aboard would be like.
Admission: Adults £15.50, Child free (2014 prices)

Other Attractions

Battersea Park Children's Zoo

Battersea Park, Chelsea, Embankment SW11 4NJ
www.batterseaparkzoo.co.uk
Nearest train station: Queenstown Rd Battersea

Battersea Park is a good area for kids, with a paddling pool and large open spaces and playgrounds. It also has a zoo.

Hamleys Toy Shop

188-196 Regent St, Soho, London W1B 5BT
www.hamleys.com
Nearest tube station: Regent St

It was established in 1760 and has 7 floors packed full of the latest games. Although it's very hard to leave empty handed!

London Zoo

Outer Circle, Regent's Park, NW1 4RY
www.zsl.org/zsl-london-zoo
Nearest tube station: Regents Park

This has a wide variety of animals and activities for the kids to do. It is also next to Regents Park which is central and good to roam around.

Sea Life London Aquarium

Riverside Building, Westminster Bridge Rd, SE1 7PB
www.visitsealife.com/london
Nearest tube station: Waterloo/Westminster

This can take a few hours, it's quite big. It has sharks, jellyfish, penguins and many interactive activities and is located just next to Westminster.

Skateboard Park - Southbank

www.londonskateparks.co.uk/skateparks/southbank
Nearest tube station: Waterloo

Teenagers can watch the daring cyclists and skateboarders from the river. Although this area is under threat now from development.

Walk from Big Ben to the Tate Modern and beyond

Start at Big Ben, cross the river, turn left, past the London Eye, the Barbican Centre and South Bank, stop off at the Tate Modern with its fantastic Turbine Hall entrance, then onto to London Bridge and over the river again to the Tower of London.

West End Theatres

Nearest tube station: Leicester Square/Covent Garden/Picadilly Circus

The West End has several shows that are for kids and adults alike. Although

Sea Life London Aquarium

tickets are often expensive, if you like musicals these can be spectacular and make a special day out.

London Parks

Coram's Fields

93 Guildford Street, WC1N 1DN
Nearest tube station: Russell Square

A 7 acre playground in central London, adults are only permitted with a child and no dogs, glass or bicycles allowed.

Hampstead Heath

Nearest rail station: Hampstead Heath

A huge park, 320 hectares, not central but with plenty or space to fly a kit or run around. Good views from Parliament Hill.

Hyde Park

London W2 2UH
Nearest tube station: Hyde Park Corner/Knightsbridge/Lancaster Gate
www.royalparks.org.uk/parks/hyde-park

This is a huge park, right in the centre, with a lake, meadow and paths all around for cycling or skating.

Regent's Park

Chester Rd, London NW1 4NR
Nearest tube station: Regent's Park

Designed by John Nash in 1811. It has lovely rose gardens in the summer, and a large outdoor sports area for football, softball, rugby and cricket.

Richmond Park

Richmond, Greater London TW10 5HS
Nearest tube station: Richmond Station and then 371 or 65 bus.

2000 acres of grassland, trees and home to free roaming deer. Good cycle paths and power kiting. Great views from the top of the hill.

St James's Park

Horse Guards Road, London SW1A 2BJ
Nearest tube station: St Jame's Park

Near the Royal Palaces, a smaller park, with a lake with pelicans (watch them being fed at 2.30pm). This is the area to find Horse Guards Parade and the Mall, with the famous guards that keep very still. It is also near Downing Street and well known landmarks.

Theme Parks

Chessington World of Adventure

Leatherhead Rd, Chessington, Surrey KT9 2NE
Tel: 0871 663 4477
www.chessington.com
Nearest train station: Chessington South (10 minutes walk)

12 miles from London on the A243. It is closed during winter. Theme park with rides for kids of all ages.

Jurassic Encounter Adventure Golf

World of Golf, Beverley Way, New Malden, Surrey KT3 4PH
Tel: 020 8949 9200
www.jurassicencounter.com
Prehistoric themed course.

Legoland Windsor

Winkfield Rd, Windsor SL4 4AY
Tel: 0871 222 2001
www.legoland.co.uk
Nearest train station: Windsor
It has three rollercoasters and six water rides, including Spinning Spider, Laser Raiders, Vikings River Splash and more.

Thorpe Park

Staines Rd, Chertsey, Surrey KT16 8PN
Tel: 0871 663 1673
www.thorpepark.com
Nearest train station: Staines (take 950 shuttle link Bus)
Aimed at older children and adults, but plenty for all with five water rides and five rollercoasters.

Eating Out

Carluccios

Garrick Street, Covent Garden, London, WC2E 9BH
Tel: 020 7836 0990
www.carluccios.com
Nearest tube station: Covent Garden
The kids menu is a miniature version of the adult menu and comes with crayons, puzzles and games.

Skate boarding at the Southbank Centre

Giraffe

Several London locations, including 7 Kensington High St, London W8 5NP
Behind the Royal Festival Hall, Riverside Level 1, Southbank Centre, Belvedere Rd, London SE1 8XX
Tel: 020 7042 6900N
www.giraffe.net
This has friendly service and a big kids menu and activity kit.

Leon

73-76 Strand, London WC2R 0DE
3 Spital Square, London E1 5DW
12 Ludgate Circus, London EC4M 7LQ
www.leonrestaurants.co.uk
Nutritious food, a good range of children's meals, like meatballs and rice box and sweet potato falafel. The kids menu comes with an activity pack.

Rainforest Café

20-24 Shaftesbury Ave, London W1D 7EU
Tel: 020 7434 3111
www.therainforestcafe.co.uk
Nearest tube station: Piccadilly Circus
Fun jungle-themed decorations and moving guerillas and animals. The menu is average, and it can have loud birthday parties.

Sticky Fingers

1a Phillimore Gardens, Kensington, W8 7QG
Tel: 020 79385338
www.stickyfingers.co.uk
Nearest tube station: High St Kensington
Bill Wyman's (from the Rolling Stones) American-themed restaurant. Kids menu has fruit kebabs, burgers and fish

Tips for Travelling Around London with Kids

- Stay in one area for most of the day, or around central London if you want the biggest tourist spots.

- If you have a buggy, check ahead on the Transport for London website on which stations have lifts. If there is not a lift, it may be better to use the bus.

- Avoid rush hour.

- If you do take the tube, be careful with young ones and hold their hands getting on and off. They are very regular so if there is too much of a rush there will always be a next one.

- London Taxi Cabs will fit in the whole family, and although more expensive can save your sanity at the end of the day if buses are late/it's raining.

- Be realistic about how much travelling or walking a child, or teenager, or even you can handle.

- Some of the shops and streets of London are interesting days out in themselves. A walk along Oxford Street in the Christmas Lights seeing the window displays can be festive sight. Even if it is incredibly busy. The shops are a teenagers delight. Fortnum and Mason, Hamleys and Harrods have great displays and exotic foods and magical games. Fun if your kids are prepared to leave without hassling you to buy half the shop! Portobello and other markets can be fun too.

There are many services that can make a parents life a bit easier. This chapter contains a list of essential information on travel, healthcare, money, benefits and more.

Having kids can open up another world. It can start when expecting your first baby, or considering fostering or adoption. This section lists maternity services, antenatal classes, pregnancy yoga and beyond.

Maternity activities include everything from aquanatal swims (a great way of feeling less huge when pregnant), to hypnotherapy to prepare and build confidence for the birth.

If you have children and need childcare, there are also many options, from nannies to childminders, nurseries and holiday care. Ofsted and Brighton and Hove City Council both have good up to date lists of providers.

Teenagers may be worried about exams and futures, or may be attached to that Xbox. There is information on all these issues.

After all that you may wonder if there is any time left for you, so check out the section on Time Out for Parents and Carers.

If you need parenting advice or have general concerns, there is a Support and Advice section. Whether is is money advice, looking for help with teenagers, mental health issues, single parenting, travel tips, local groups if you have twins and support if your child has special needs.

USEFUL INFORMATION

BUMP TO BABY

From thinking about wanting to have a baby, to becoming pregnant and being a first time parent can be quite a journey. Your GP or information from the NHS is the first contact if you are trying to con-

ceive or are pregnant. In addition, in Brighton and Hove there are a huge range of antenatal classes and support. This chapter lists local services and sources of support on every stage of that journey.

Maternity Care

When you first suspect that you are pregnant, visit your local health centre or GP who will then be able to explain your maternity or 'antenatal' care. You will be offered appointments to check your progress and offer advice. You will also be offered antenatal classes and breastfeeding workshops. All hospitals offer at least two ultrasound scans during pregnancy, the

first around 8-14 weeks, or 'dating scan', and the second between 18 and 21 weeks 'anomaly scan'.

NHS Choices

NHS Choices has a wealth of information on pregnancy, maternity services, the birth and early years. www.nhs.uk/Conditions/pregnancy-and-baby

Maternity Units

The Royal Sussex County Hospital and Princess Royal Hospital are the main maternity services in Brighton and Hove. You can usually choose to have your baby in a hospital, a midwife-led unit or at home, depending on your health and your pregnancy. Expectant mothers are looked after in a single room at Level 13 of the Tower Block at the Royal Sussex or the second floor at the Princess Royal. For further information on maternity services, visit their website 'My Pregnancy Matters'. www.mypregnancymatters.co.uk

There is also a **Brighton and Hove Maternity Services Liaison Committee.** This is an independent organisation run by parents for parents. It gives support and information on pregnancy, birth and afterwards. www.brightonandhovemslc.com

Royal Sussex County Hospital

Eastern Road, Brighton BN2 5BE
Tel: 01273 696955
Delivery Suite - 01273 664793
Antenatal Clinic - 01273 696955 Ext. 4392
Postnatal Ward - 01273 696955 Ext. 4368
Trevor Mann Baby Unit - 01273 696955 Ext. 4377
Community Midwives - 01273 664794

Princess Royal Hospital

Lewes Road, Haywards Heath
West Sussex RH16 4EX
Tel: 01444 441881
Delivery Suite - 01444 448669
Antenatal Clinic - 01444 441881 Ext. 8413
Day Assessment Unit - 01444 441881 Ext. 5486
Bolney Ward - 01444 441881 Ext. 8479
Special Care Baby Unit - 01444 441881 Ext. 8489

Visiting times for maternity

Royal Sussex County Hospital maternity:
Partners and own children: 10am–1pm and 3pm–8pm
General visiting: 3pm–8pm

Princess Royal Hospital maternity:

Partners and own children: 10am–1pm and 2pm–9pm
General visiting: 2pm–4pm and 7pm–8pm
www.bsuh.nhs.uk/departments/maternity-services-and-labour-wards

East Sussex Maternity Services

There are three main centres that service East Sussex, which care for around 4,200 women a year. Midwifery-led care is available at GP surgeries, children's centres and at the three hospitals below. Consultant-led care is provided at the Conquest Hospital.
East Sussex maternity services website:
www.esh.nhs.uk/maternity

Eastbourne District General Hospital

Kings Drive, Eastbourne
East Sussex, BN21 2UD
Tel: 01323 417400
www.esh.nhs.uk/hospitals/eastbournedgh/

Worthing Hospital

Lyndhurst Road, Worthing
West Sussex BN11 2DH
Tel: 01903 205111

Crowborough Birthing Centre

Southview Road, Crowborough
Sussex TN6 1HB
Tel: 01892 652284

Lewes and East Sussex Antenatal

NCT Bumps & Babies

Lewes YMCA, Fri 10am – noon, coordinator.lewesandcountryside@nct.org.uk

NCT Eastbourne & District

General enquiries: Eastbourne@nct.org.uk, antenatal classes:, Tel: 0844 2436913

NCT, Lewes & Countryside

Tel: 0208 7529106
coordinator.lewesandcountryside@nct.org.uk

The Muma Baby Sanctuary

32 Cliffe High St., Lewes BN7 2AN
mumababysanctuary@gmail.com
http://mumababysanctuary.co.uk/
Sharon - Tel: 07771 928 271
Samsara - Tel: 07838 136 715

Baby Sign - Sing and Sign

Christ Church Lewes, Prince Edwards Road, Lewes, East Sussex, BN7 1BL
Tel: 01273 243786
www.singandsign.com/classes/classes-near-you/lewes-uckfield-ringmer-haywards-heath-peacehaven

Antenatal Classes

There are so many antenatal classes on offer that there are too many to list here. Some of these book up quickly, so it pays to have a look early in pregnancy to see if you'd like to join any. It can be a great way of getting to know other people who are due at the same time. They usually cover health in pregnancy, what happens during birth, caring for and feeding your baby.

All first time parents are offered three antenatal classes free from the NHS to prepare for their birth, feeding and the first days with their new baby. Your community midwife can advise on local availability. They usually begin 8-10 weeks before your baby is due.

Most antenatal classes are open to women and men, and can be a a good way to share experiences. There are also many classes especially for pregnant mothers, such as yoga, relax and floating and hypnotherapy in preparation for birth.

Here are a few of the services provided but there are many more, have a browse for yourself.

0-6 months - Parent Skool
Tel: 01273 841101
Email: info@parentskool.co.uk
www.parentskool.co.uk
Billed as a 'crash course in having a baby', these are aimed at those early days with a baby, giving support and advice on feeding, sleeping, crying and what to buy. There are practical exercises using life size baby dolls.

Brighton Natural Health Centre
Based in the North Laine, Brighton, it runs Pregnancy and Mums and Babies classes. Pregnancy Yoga is for women who are more than 14 weeks' pregnant.
www.bnhc.co.uk

National Childbirth Trust (NCT)
East Sussex BN1 1YA
Tel 01273 685692
Main branch contact:
Tel: 08442436062
brightonhovenct@yahoo.co.uk
Antenatal and postnatal classes:
www.facebook.com/#!/pages/NCT-Brighton-Hove/127904093893451
www.freedom-leisure.co.uk
This has a local branch run by volunteers and offers support for parents and those who are pregnant. It can be a good way of getting to know local parents. Brighton and Hove offer monthly play sessions on the first Sunday of every month, antenatal courses, weaning workshops, relax and float classes. For details of courses:
Tel: 0844 243 6062 option 4 (Claire) or email bookings4o@nct.org.uk
There are also 3 nearly new sales a year, cafe baby (BN3), home birth support and open house coffee mornings.
Other support:
National Helpline 0300 330 0700
Postnatal Helpline 0300 300 0773

Sussex HypnoBirthing
Tel: 01273 385 370
Email: info@sussexhypnobirthing.com
http://sussexhypnobirthing.com
Self hypnosis with childbirth education. It aims to help with being relaxed through labour and birth.

Yoga Mamas
Tel: 07908949419
hello@yogamamas.co.uk
http://yogamamas.co.uk/pregnancy/
Yoga Mamas's founder, Clare Maddalena, has created 'LushTums Pregnancy Yoga Classes' now running all across Brighton & Hove & Sussex.

Aqua Natal

At the later stages of pregnancy being in a pool floating around may offer some welcome relief. Sessions are offered at the King Alfred, the Prince Regent and at Little Dippers.

King Alfred
Kingsway, Hove,
East Sussex BN3 2WW
Tel: 01273 290290
kingalfredenquiries@freedom-leisure.co.uk
www.freedom-leisure.co.uk

Little Dippers Pool
42 Upper Gardner St
Brighton BN1 3AN
Tel: 0844 482 0222
www.littledippers.co.uk
Little Dippers have baby swimming in a purpose built baby pool.

St Luke's Swimming Pool
St Luke's Terrace, Brighton BN2 9ZE
Tel: 01273 602385
www.freedom-leisure.co.uk

Prince Regent Swimming Complex
Church Street Brighton BN1 1YA
Tel: 01273 685692
www.freedom-leisure.co.uk

Twins Antenatal and Postnatal Classes

Brighton and Hove NHS Trust supported and cared for 131 sets of twins and 4 sets of triplets in 2013. Multiple births occur in about 1 in 65 women. There are specific antenatal classes from the NHS free for those expecting twins or more. They also list the following antenatal classes:

Salvation Army Twins Group
Fridays 9:45am to 11:45am (Term Time Only).
Sheila 01273 607095

Friends with Twins:
Every Fortnight on Thursdays at Saltdean Lido Lower Hall from 10 am to 12:30pm.
Ceri on 07541564334 or Nicole 07811078320

Moulscoomb Children's Centre
Hodshrove Lane, Brighton BN2 4SE
1st Wednesday of every Month 2.30pm-4pm .

Conway Court Children's Centre
Hove BN3 3WR
Friday 2pm -3.30pm

Hangleton Park Chidren's Centre
Harmsworth Crescent BN3 3BW
Monday 9.30 -11.30am

Worthing
www.twinsandtriplets.co.uk.

Fortnightly. Goring United Reform church

Post Natal - Keep Fit, Yoga & Movies

Baby & Mama Postnatal Yoga Classes
121-123 Davigdor Rd, Hove, East Sussex, BN3 1RE
Tel: 07912 443 998
info@yoga2shape.com
www.yoga2shape.com

Baby & Me Massage & Relax Classes Yoga Mamas Studio, 40-42 Upper Gardner Street, Brighton BN1
Tel: 07773 063273
sonia@sussexhypnobirthing.com
www.sussexhypnobirthing.com

Baby & Postnatal Yoga
Dyke Road Natural Health Clinic, 274 Dyke Road, Brighton, BN1 5AE
Tel: 01273 479303
daisymay90@hotmail.com
www.dykeroadclinic.co.uk
Babies from 6 weeks to crawling.

Bring-your-baby Zumba!
Ralli Hall, Denmark Villas, Hove, BN3 3TH
zumbabyjennyc@gmail.com
Tel: 07921628522
www.facebook.com/groups/zumbabyjennyc
A Zumba class for mums where babies are welcome. Tuesday mornings. £6 per class drop in.

Pure Aerobics Classes with crèche
Hangleton Community Centre, Harmsworth Crescent, Hove, BN3 8BW
christine@pureaerobicsbrighton.co.uk
First Class Free; 3 sessions for £10 Termtime only. Aerobics classes with creche provided in Hove. Children are looked after by qualified nanny. in Tiny Tims soft play room.

Ready Steady Mums

Hove Park and Preston Park, BN3 6BE
marine@readysteadymums.com
http://readysteadymums.com
Free local buggy exercise group. Alternates between Hove Park and Preston Park.

The Big Scream - Cinema
Duke of York's Picturehouse, Preston Circus, Brighton BN1 4NA
Tel: 0871 902 5728
www.picturehouses.co.uk/cinema/Duke_Of_Yorks/Whats_On/Clubs_Groups/Big_Scream
£7.60 Thu, 11am (doors open 10.30am). Weekly shows of films for adults to watch, in the morning for carers of babies under 1 year.

Adoption & Fostering

Brighton & Hove City Council
Tel: 01273 295444
www.fosteringinbrightonandhove.org.uk
You can obtain an information pack from Brighton & Hove City Council, which has comprehensive information if you are considering fostering or adopting a child.

Single Parents

Spin Brighton
http://groupspaces.com/spinbrighton
Information network of single parents with sole or shared care of their children in Brighton and Hove and surrounding areas providing regular emails to members plus support, advice, opportunities for meetups and events via their Facebook group.

Brighton Women's Centre
Brighthelm Centre North Road Brighton, BN1 1YD
Tel: 01273 749 567
www.womensaid.org.uk
The Centre's drop-in facility in central Brighton offers a range of facilities including information and support, a li-

brary, counselling, free pregnancy testing and Toybox pre-school.

Brighton Single Parent Socials
www.meetup.com/Single-Parents Brighton
Forum for single parents to find like minded people to enjoy nature, sport and the arts.

Gingerbread
Tel: (Freephone Helpline) 0800 802 0925
www.gingerbread.org.uk
National support group, for advice and information.

Baby & Toddler Groups

There are a large number of baby and toddler groups in Brighton and Hove. Your local children's centre, church and community centre may well have a session. They are usually for an hour, where you can stay with your baby or toddler and meet other parents and carers. Most places provide toys and somewhere to play, and others music or activities. There is baby yoga, baby swimming, baby signing to name a few! It it worthwhile checking the Libraries section too for the rhymetimes and storytimes for preschool children. There are too many to list so this is just a sample. And please bear in mind that times and places are subject to change, so always check with each provider first.

Baby and Beyond Baby Massage
West Werks, 41-43 Portland Road,
Hove, East Sussex, BN3 5DQ
Tel: 01273 702496
info@tobabyandbeyond.com
www.tobabyandbeyond.com

Baby Sensory
brightoncentral@babysensory.co.uk
Tel: 07926 248 639
www.babysensory.com/en/ClassDetails
/brighton-central
Room with lights, glowing bouncy
balls, bubbles, bells, puppets and
tickly feathers.

Baby Swimming
Little Dippers Pool, 42 Upper Gardner
St, Brighton BN1 3AN
Tel: 0844 482 0222
www.littledippers.co.uk
Little Dippers have baby swimming in
a purpose built baby pool.

Music Bugs
Brighton, Hove, Peacehaven, Lewes,
East Sussex
Tel: 0844 822 1174
kelly@musicbugs.co.uk
www.musicbugs.co.uk/location/brighto
n-and-eastbourne/
3 months to 4 years. Music, singing,
toys and paradchutes.

Sensory Baby Hub Classes
West Hill Hall, Compton Ave, Seven
Dials, Brighton and Hove, East Sussex,
BN13PS
Tel: 01273736823
monique@sensorybabyhub.co.uk
www.sensorybabyhub.co.uk
Babies early communication skills
while developing sensory and body
awareness.

Sing & Sign
Brighton & Hove,
Tel: 01273 540266
info@singandsign.co.uk
www.singandsign.co.uk
Includes half an hour of singing and
signing as well as social time.

Sussex Central YMCA
17 Marmion Road, Hove BN3 5FS
Tel: 01273 715439
Mondays, Wednesdays and Fridays 9.30
– 12pm
Toddlers Gym. Fun, free play
sessions, lots of play equipment and
bouncy castle for the under 4s.£3.00

The Crypt Parent and Baby Group
Kemp Town Crypt Community Centre,
St. Georges Church, St. Georges Road,
Brighton BN2 1ED
Tel: 01273 290300
Health visitor run baby group.

TigerTots Baby & Preschool Gymnastics
The Fulbourn Centre, Home End,
Fulbourn, Cambridge CB21 5BS
Tel: 07775 853123
tigertots@ntlworld.com
www.tigertots.co.uk
Suitable for babies as young as 8
weeks, preschool gymnastics is a foundation for children's natural physical
development.

Drop-in baby groups

There are many children's centres
that offer drop in sessions.

West Hove Children's Centre
School Road, Hove
Tel: 01273 733386 / 266011
First-time parents, carers and pre-
crawling babies.

Cornerstone Community Centre
Church Road, Hove, BN3 2FL
Tel 01273 294111

Roundabout Childrens Centre
Whitehawk Road, Brighton BN2 5FL
Tel 01273 290300
Crawling and newly walking babies.

Conway Court Children's Centre
Clarendon Road, Hove BN3 3WR
Tel: 01273 266011
Drop-in for pre-crawling babies.

Hangleton Park Children's Centre
Harmsworth Crescent, Hove
Tel: 01273 295272

Home-Start
This voluntary scheme offers
friendship, support and
practical help to families with
children under five years old.
It is particularly for those
families struggling to cope.
Available in certain areas
around Sussex.

East Sussex Home Start
30a High Street, Newhaven, East
Sussex, BN9 9PD
Tel: 01273 612025
info@homestartsouthdowns.org.uk
www.homestartsouthdowns.org.uk

Moulsecoomb Children's Centre
Hodshrove Lane, Brighton
Tel: 01273 294040
Pre-crawling/pre-walking babies.

North Portslade Children's Centre
The Rise, Portslade
Tel: 01273 294062
Pre-crawling/pre-walking babies.

Hollingdean Children's Centre
Brentwood Road, Brighton
Tel: 01273 295623
Pre-crawling/pre-walking babies.

Hollingbury and Patcham Children's Centre
Carden CP School, County Oak
Avenue, Brighton BN1 8LU
Tel: 01273 293311
Pre-crawling/pre-walking babies.

Roundabout Children's Centre
Whitehawk Road, Brighton
Tel: 01273 290300
Pre-crawling/pre-walking babies.

Tarner Children's Centre
Ivory Place, Brighton BN2 9QE
Tel: 01273 296700
Pre-walking babies (birth to 8 months).

TIME OUT FOR PARENTS & CARERS

Being a carer of children, particularly young children, can be a demanding job. It can be hard to take time off to take care of yourself. If you are able to get some time off.

Try a spa treatment, or local leisure centres have steam rooms for a cheaper option, such as the Prince Regent Swimming Complex. If you want to keep in shape, there are some gyms with an attached crèche.

If you are missing the cinema and have a baby, there are special 'Big Scream' screenings at local cinemas. Longer term, you may be considering your career, re-training or volunteering. If you are a single parent, it can be even harder to get time off, however there are support groups locally (page 92).

Pampering & Relaxation

Asase Spa The Lanes
Hanningtons, unit 13
19 Brighton Pl, Brighton
Tel: 01273 746888

The Grand Hotel Brighton
97-99 King's Road, Brighton BN1 2FW
Tel: 08712 224 684
www.grandbrighton.co.uk/spa-en.html

Little Jasmine Therapies and Spa
14 New Rd, Brighton
Tel: 01273 911500
www.little-jasmine.com

Photo via Wikimedia Commons

The Treatment Rooms
21 New Rd, Brighton
Tel: 01273 818444
www.thetreatmentrooms.com

Babysitters

It is not easy to find someone that you trust to mind your child. If you decide to get a babysitter, whether a friend, family or professional service, consider their experience, whether they have first aid training, how they will play, deal with a tantrum or problem with your child. Ask for references and follow these up. You will need to decide if they are responsible enough to look after your child and handle an emergency. The NSPCC recommends only using registered childminders.
www.nspcc.org.uk/help-and-advice/for-parents/keeping-your-child-safe

Ofsted
www.ofsted.gov.uk
For a list of registered childminders.

Gyms with a Crèche

Alive Fitness & Natural Health Ltd
22-27 Castle Street, Sussex Brighton, BN1 2HD
www.alivehealth.co.uk

Independent gym very centrally located. It has a sauna, cardio machines, weights and resistance machines. Crèche on Monday to Saturday mornings. For 3 months to 8 years for up to 2 hours per day.

Impulse Leisure Southwick
Old Barn Way, Southwick,
West Sussex BN42 4NT
Tel: 01273 238111
www.impulseleisure.co.uk/southwick-home
In Southwick Leisure Centre , fitness suite, cardiovascular and resistance equipment. It has a cafe. The creche takes children from 3 months to 5 years, on Monday to Friday mornings.

Prince Regent Swimming Complex
Church Street Brighton BN1 1YA
Tel: 01273 685692
www.brighton-hove.gov.uk/content/leisure-and-libraries/sports-and-activity/prince-regent-swimming-complex
Swimming pool and fully equipped gym, sauna and steam room. Supervised non-registered crèche. Operates three sessions each week Tuesday 9.00-10.45, Thursday 9.30—11 and Friday 10.15-12

Splashpoint Leisure Centre
60 Brighton road, BN11 2EN, Worthing BN11 2EN
Tel: 01903 502237
www.worthingleisure.co.uk/junior-activities/creche
3 indoor pools, a huge gym, two fitness studios, cafe and outdoor

paddling pool. The creche is Ofsted registered and situated at Worthing Leisure Centre. All sessions must be pre-booked, on Monday to Friday mornings.

Movies

Staying in is the new going out! Well, it can be, if you have young children and limited or zero babysitting. However there are DVD rentals, box sets and satellite TV on demand features so that you can still see the latest movies at home. There is also the 'Big Scream', where you can watch a movie in a cinema if you are a parent with a baby under one.

Arts Picture House Brighton - Big Scream

Preston Circus, Brighton BN1 4NA
Tel 0871 902 5728
www.picturehouses.co.uk/cinema/Duke_Of_Yorks/Whats_On/Clubs_Groups/Big_Scream/
Low lights are left on and nappy changing facilities for these movies exclusively for parents with babies under one year old. Wednesday mornings - check website. See page 17.

DVD Rentals & Satellite Options

There are so many options, and special offers these days. Check out www.moneysavingexpert.com for the best deals.

Education and Training

Adult Careers Advice East Sussex

www.eastsussex.gov.uk/jobs/ideas/help.htm
Useful website with a list of organisations to help with careers, education or finding work.

Brighton Unemployed Centre

6 Tilbury Place, Brighton, BN2 0GY
Tel : 01273 671213 / 601211
www.bucfp.org
The Centre was set up in 1981. Brighton Unemployed Centre Families Project became a registered charity in 1994 and is run by the unemployed for the unemployed. We provide practical support, education and recreation for those in poor housing, claimants, unwaged people and those on low incomes.

Evening Argus News Jobs

www.theargus.co.uk
Jobs in Brighton and Hove every Thursday.

National Careers Service

nationalcareersservice.direct.gov.uk
Provides advice and support on careers.

Open University

www.open.ac.uk
Distance learning, with flexible options which can fit around children.

Working Links

4-20 Pavilion Parade, Brighton BN1 1EB
Tel: 012373 766427
www.workinglinks.co.uk/office_finder/office_finder.aspx
A free programme which provides help with job searching, such as applications, organising childcare and interview technique training. If you live in Brighton & Hove and are a lone parent, then Working Links Lone Parent Back to Work Programme is tailored for your needs.

Volunteering

Volunteer Centre Brighton & Hove

Second Floor, Community Base
113 Queens Road, Brighton BN1 3XG
Tel: 01273 737888
www.volunteering.org.uk
Helps to match people who want to volunteer with organisations needing volunteers.

CHILDCARE & SCHOOLS
IN BRIGHTON & HOVE

There are a wide range of childcare providers in Brighton and the surrounding area. You may want to talk to other parents, check reports on Ofsted and visit a few before making your choice.

Nannies provide care in your own home, childminders in their own home. Childminders are registered with Ofsted, nannies do not, at present have to be registered. An au pair is a cultural exchange programme where young people abroad can live with you and learn about the UK in exchange for light household duties.

If you have a pre-school toddler, local playgroups are a good way to meet other parents and provide kids with a child friendly environment outside of home. There are also Children's Centres which provide support and advice for parents of 0-5yrs in certain areas.

Children from households receiving particular benefits may be entitled to some free childcare from two years old. All three and four year olds become eligible for free early learning places from the school term after their third birthday. This is 15 free hours per week over 38 weeks.

Brighton and Hove City Council has information on choosing childcare and a useful childcare directory.
www.brighton-hove.gov.uk/content/children-and-education/information-and-advice-families/choosing-childcare

You may be eligible for Tax Credits, which help meet the cost of childcare if you qualify. The two information sites below can give more advice.

GOV.UK
www.gov.uk/browse/benefits/tax-credits
Citizens Advice Brighton & Hove
www.citizensadvice.org.uk/brightonhovecab.htm

Children's Centres in Brighton & Hove

These are useful centres of advice, support, playgroups and more. You can contact the Brighton & Hove City Council's family information service to find out more on 01273 293545.

www.brighton-hove.gov.uk/content/children-and-education/childrens-services/childrens-centres

Tarner Children's Centre in partnership with Tarnerland Nursery
Ivory Place, Brighton, BN2 9QE
Tel: 01273 296700

Cornerstone Community & CC
Church Road, Hove, BN3 2FL
Tel: 01273 327757

Hollingbury & Patcham Gateway CC
Carden School, County Oak Ave, Brighton BN1 8LU
Tel: 01273 293311

Hollingdean Children's Centre & Cherry Tree Nursery
Brentwood Rd, Brighton BN1 7DY
Tel: 01273 295623

City View Gateway CC
Brighton General Hospital, Elm Grove, Brighton, BN2 3EW
Tel: 01273 242225

North Portslade CC & Acorn Nursery
The Rise, Portslade, BN41 2PY
Tel: 01273 294062

South Portslade CC & Library
223 Old Shoreham Road, Portslade, BN41 1XR

Ofsted

www.ofsted.gov.uk

Ofsted is the Office for Standards in Education, Children's Services and Skills. It inspects and regulates services which care for children, such as child minders, nurseries and schools. You can find an inspection report by looking on their website.

You may also want to look at the history of providers who previously operated from the same site. These closed providers may or may not have a relationship with the current provision in terms of management or ownership. Providers cannot start caring for children until they have a certificate of registration.

Tel: 01273 296895

Conway Court CC in partnership with Honeycroft pre-school
Clarendon Rd, Hove, BN3 3WR
Tel: 01273 266011

West Hove Gateway CC
West Hove Infants School Portland Rd, Hove, BN3 5JA
Tel: 01273 733386

Hangleton Park Gateway CC
Harmsworth Crescent, Hangleton, BN3 8BW
Tel: 01273 295272

Moulsecoomb CC & Jump Start Nursery
Hodshrove Lane, Brighton, BN2 4SE
Tel: 01273 294040

Bevendean Gateway CC
Bevendean Primary School, Heath Hill Avenue, Brighton, BN2 4JP
Tel: 01273 696347

Roundabout CC and Nursery
Whitehawk Road, Brighton, BN2 5FL
Tel: 01273 290300

The Deans Gateway CC
Rudyard Kipling School, Chalkland Rise, Woodingdean, Brighton BN2 6RH
Tel: 01273 306387

Westdene Gateway CC
Westdene Primary School, Bankside, Brighton, BN1 5GN
Tel: 01273 293311

Fairlight Gateway CC
Fairlight Primary & Nursery School, St Leonards Road, Brighton, BN2 3AJ
Tel: 01273 242225

Preston Park Gateway CC
At Fiveways Play Centre, between 8-10 Florence Road, Brighton, BN1 6DJ
Tel: 01273 500257

Lewes Children's Centre
Malling Community Centre , Spences Lane, Lewes BN7 2HQ
Tel: 01273 336870

Au Pairs

The au pair programme is a cultural exchange where a person from abroad is expected to be welcomed as a member your family and be given their own room. Traditionally, an au pair would be 18 to 27 years old, and can be on duty from 25-35 hours per week. The au pair would be given an allowance, minimum £75 per week.

There is an expectation that the au pair would attend language lessons and time off. This is in addition to light housework and helping with children and they are not permitted to have continuous sole charge of children under 2. The British Au Pair Agencies Association provides guidelines for employing au pairs. www.bapaa.org.uk

Childminders

They are self-employed childcare professionals who work from their own home. They care for smaller numbers, and it is more 'home from home'. Childminders who look after children under eight years for more than two hours a day have to be registered with Ofsted and hold a certificate. A list of registered childminders is available on the their website. The Family Information Directory from Brighton & Hove City Council also has a list of registered childminders:

Childcare Information Team
www.brighton-hove.gov.uk/content/children-and-education/information-and-advice-families/choosing-childcare

Professional Association for Childcare and Early Years (PACEY)
PO Box 209, Royston, Herts SG8 0AN
Tel: 01223 207984
Deborah.Townsend@pacey.org.uk
www.pacey.org.uk
Formerly known as The National Childminding Association (NCMA)) PACEY provides information to help find childcare.

Nannies

Nannies are employed by parents to work in the child's own home. The child can form a close relationship and siblings can be looked after together. Nannies can be flexible, possibly offering evening babysitting and you don't have to travel to the childcare setting.

However, unlike childminders nannies do not need to be registered by Ofsted or have specific training.

Playgroups

Pre-school playgroup are generally less formal than nurseries and open for a few hours a day rather than full time. Usually the parent is expected to stay with their child. It is a good opportunity to meet other local parents. There are groups listed in the Ofsted and Brighton & Hove City Council website. There are more playgroups run by your local Children's Centre so it is also worth getting in touch with them if they are near you.

Playbus

www.brighton-hove.gov.uk/content/children-and-education/information-and-advice-families/playbus
The Brighton & Hove playbus travels around the area providing play activities all year round. The service is free.

Baby and Toddler Groups

Pre-school playgroup are generally less formal than nurseries and open for a few hours a day rather than full time. Usually the parent is expected to stay with their child. It is a good opportunity to meet other local parents. There are 45 groups listed in the excellent Brighton and Hove City Council Family Directory, from music to singing, football to baby gyms. See also the Bump to Baby chapter for a list of baby and toddler playgroups.
www.brighton-hove.gov.uk/fis
www.familyinfobrighton.org.uk

Day Nurseries

These are childcare services which usually offer full-time care, usually from 8am to 6pm, for children from 3 months to 5 years. They usually operate all year round. Most offer the free early education places that are avvailable to all 3 and 4 year olds, and from September 2013, some two year olds. They are registered with OFSTED and you can find reports on their website.

Holiday Play Schemes and After School

The excellent City Council Family Information Service provides a good **Summer Fun booklet** listing activities and holidays camps in Brighton and Hove.
familyinfo@brighton-hove.gov.uk
Tel: 01273 293545
www.brighton-hove.gov.uk/content/children-and-education/information-and-advice-families/activities-children-and-young-people

The Sports Development Team - offers a wide range of sport and physical activity with strong links to local clubs, coaches and organisations and the opportunity to continue with your chosen activity all year round.
Tel: 01273 292721
holidaysportcourses@brighton-hove.gov.uk
www.brighton-hove.gov.uk/holidaysports

The University of Sussex
www.sussex.ac.uk/sport/children

Offers high quality coaching using their very good facilities, for 5 to 16 year olds.

Beach Sports Amigos Summer Scheme

Cornerstone Community Centre, Church Road, Hove
www.amigospreschool.btck.co.uk

Boomerang Kids

Saltdean Barn, Saltdean Oval Park, Arundel Drive West, Saltdean
www.boomerang-kids.co.uk

Barracudas Day Camps

Patcham High School,
Ladies Mile Road, Patcham
www.barracudas.co.uk

Brighton & Hove Inclusion Project (BHIP)

West Blatchington Primary and Nursery School, Hangleton Way, Hove
www.bhip.org.uk

Montessori Holiday Club

67 Stanford Avenue, Brighton
www.brighton-montessori.org.uk

extratime

www.extratimebrighton.org.uk
Fun, stimulating, safe, inclusive environments. For children with and without disabilities.

Pied Piper Activities

Lancing Prep, The Droveway Hove
www.piedpipreactivities.co.uk
Fun packed multi-activity camp.

Super Camps

Brighton & Hove High School
Radinden Manor Road, Hove
www.supercamps.co.uk

The Academies

Brighton College, Eastern Road, Brighton
www.theacademies.co.uk

Queen's Park Summer Playscheme

Freshfield Place, Brighton
www.queenspark.brighton-hove.sch.uk/extended services

Tarnerland Play Scheme

Tarnerland Playbase, Sussex Street, Brighton
www.tarnerland.org.uk

Care of Children With Disabilities and Special Needs

You may need more tailored care for your child. Childminders and nannies have the advantage of being more flexible and home-based. Day Nurseries can also offer specialised care. It may be worth investigating a variety of options and talking to local support groups to find the best care for your child. There is an that organisation in the local area, Amaze, that can provide support to parents, information and advice.
www.amazebrighton.org.uk

State Schools

Brighton & Hove City Council is responsible for 80 schools, of which 54 are in Brighton. State schools are free for children from the September after their fourth birthday. The school year begins in September and is divided into Autumn, Spring and Summer Terms. Apply for a place at the County Council. Primary education is for ages 4 to 11 years, Secondary education is for 11 to 16 yrs. Further education is provided in Sixth Form Colleges and Further Education Colleges.

You must apply for a place, even if your child attends the nursery of a primary school. You will probably

look for a school near to where you live. Pupils are prioritised according to the council's admission priorities.

There are deadlines for applications and it is important to get your application in on time. For primary schools the deadline for 2015 is 15 January 2015. The deadline for secondary schools was 31 October 2014 for a start in 2015. You will need to check the Council website for deadlines in subsequent years in case they change.

Brighton & Hove Council Admissions Team

Schools Admissions Team
Brighton & Hove City Council
King's House, Grand Avenue,
Hove BN3 2SU
Tel: 01273 293653
Admissions@cambridgeshire.gov.uk
www.brighton-hove.gov.uk/content/children-and-education/school-admissions

Private Schools

There are a number of private schools, including Brighton College, Roedean School, Steiner School, BHHS and a Montessori School

CHILDREN WITH SPECIAL NEEDS

If you have a child with special needs, many of the activities and places listed in this book have provisions to enable your child to attend the centre or activity. It is worth checking out their websites or contacting them in advance. For example for children sensitive to sound and light there are autism friendly cinema screenings at the Duke of Yorks cinema with lower level volume.

There are also some local organisations that are specifically geared up to children or young people with special needs. Some of these are listed here. However check with Amaze and Brighton and Hove City Couoncil for a more comprehensive list.
Amaze also hosts the PaCC, the local parent carers council where parent carers come together to have a voice on the issues that matter to them and their children. Tel: 01273 772289

Adventure Unlimited
Tel: 01273 681058
info@aultd.org
www.aultd.org
Adventure Unlimited offer fun activities indoors and out – including climbing, archery, kayaking and bush craft.

Amaze
Tel: 01273 772289
helpline@amazebrighton.org.uk
www.amazebrighton.org.uk
Amaze works with parents of children and young people with disabilities and special needs aged 0-19 in Brighton & Hove. It provides the compass card, and the hosts the local parents support group. It really does a huge amount in the area and is a very good starting place for advice, support and information on local groups, activities and advocacy.

Barnardo's Brighton and Hove Link Plus Service
Tel: 01273 295179
www.barnardos.org.uk/.../Brightonandhovelink
Recruits, trains and supports foster carers to provide care to disabled young people aged 0-18 years.

Brighton Pebbles
Brighton Pebbles is a not for profit group run by parent carers, particularly for children who find it difficult to access mainstream activities.

Photo by Ben Moore

Carousel
Tel: 01273 234734
enquiries@carousel.org.uk
www.carousel.org.uk
Activities to engage people with a learning disability in the arts. It is recognised for its high quality.

Cedar Centre
www.cedar-centre.co.uk
School for pupils aged 6 -16 with complex needs, including: moderate learning disabilities, Autistic Spectrum Conditions, ADHD, mental health and medical needs. Based in Hollingbury.

Chailey Heritage School
www.chs.org.uk
A non maintained day and residential special school for children from 3 to 19 years with complex physical disabilities and health needs.

Spiral
www.spiralsussex.co.uk
Sports activities for people with learning difficulties and disabilities, aged 14 and over. Includes swimming, basketball, youth clubs, dance, drama, and the new spiral wave radio.

Sussex Deaf Association
Tel: 01273 671899

info@sussexdeaf.co.uk
www.sussexdeaf.co.uk
Support and information, communication, befriending, and interpreting.

SWBC Tigers Sussex Wheelchair Basketball Club
stephen@swbctigers.com
www.swbctigers.com
14years and upwards. Professional coaches support the team members.

Sweet Peas Parent & Toddler group
Tel: 01273 236366
Pre-school groups for children with special needs and their families.

Portage (Children's Society)
Tel: 01273 749 085
Gives support to young disabled children up to the age of four and their families to increase their quality of life.

PRESENS (Pre School Special Educational Needs Service)
Tel: 01273 294944
presens@brighton-hove.gov.uk
Teachers and nursery nurses visit children in their nursery or home, providing support and advice..

Advocacy

ADDISS - National
Middlesex HA8 7BJ
Tel: 020 8952 2800 info@addiss.co.uk
www.addiss.co.uk
This is the national **A**ttention **D**eficit **D**isorder **I**nformation and **S**upport Service.

Schools and Education
In most cases, children with special educational needs attend mainstream schools, however for those with more complex needs a special school may be offered. In Cambridgeshire there are six area and three county-wide special schools. There are also Independent special schools.

Admissions
www.brighton-hove.gov.uk/content/children-and-education/brighton-hoves-local-offer

If you have any concerns about your child's development, your first port of call should be your health visitor, your child's teacher or your GP. They may be able to reassure you or advise you about what to do next.

Parents and carers can ask any professional who knows their child to complete a referral form and send it to the team at Seaside View Child Development Centre. Parents and carers are also welcome to contact Seaside View directly for more information.

Compass Card
Amaze provides the Compass Card. This is a leisure incentive card for children and young people aged 0 – 19 with significant special needs.

It includes free swimming, free fitness sessions for 12 to 15 yrs, free gym 16 to 19 yrs. As well as special offers on shows, theatre, soft play and main attractions.

Parenting

Bad Mothers Club
www.badmothersclub.com
'In the aisle by the chill cabinets, no-one can hear you scream.' This is the tag line of this tongue in cheek look at parenting.

Barnardo's
www.barnardos.org.uk
Parenting support through family centres and work with children.

Family Advice
www.familylives.org.uk
A parenting charity with advice and information.

Parenting Support Centre
www.parenting.co.uk

Single Parents

Support and Advice for Children

Childline
www.childline.org.uk
Tel: 0800 1111
Confidential information and advice for young people themselves on bullying, back to school and other topics.

Clock Tower Sanctuary
www.theclocktowersanctuary.org.uk
Tel: 01273 722353
Provides a drop in and referral centre for homeless young people aged 16 to 25. Food and clothing store.

NSPCC
National Society for the Protection of Children
www.nspcc.org.uk
Tel: 0808 800 5000
Text: 88858
Help@nspcc.org.uk
Help and advice if you are worried about a child, free 24 hour helpline.

SUPPORT & ADVICE

LGBT
www.allsortsyouth.org.uk
Tel: 01273 721211
A project for young people under 26 who are lesbian, gay, transgender or unsure of their sexuality.

Ru-ok?
www.areyouok.org.uk
Tel: 01273 293966

Young person's substance misuse service, up to age of 19 in the Brighton and Hove area.

Talk to Frank
www.talktofrank.com
Confidential drugs advice.

Under 25
www.allsortsyouth.org.uk
Tel: 01273 721211

A project for young people under 26 who are lesbian, gay, transgender or unsure of their sexuality.

Young Minds

www.youngminds.org.uk
Parent helpine: 0808 802 5544
Help and advice on young people's mental health and wellbeing.

Teenagers

Exams, Careers, Volunteering

Dv8 Training Brighton

www.dv8training.com
01273 55042
Dv8 provides training courses for young people who are looking to break into the creative industries. We run courses in music, media, fashion and much more.

Duke of Edinburgh's award

www.brightonandhovedea.org.uk
Tel: 01273 609746
Caters for young people between 14 and 25years.

Youth Advice Centre

www.hoveymca.org.uk
Drop in services for 13-25 year olds.

UCAS Progress

www.ucasprogress.com
A website for 14-19 year olds to find courses and training.

Youth Employability Service

Tel: 01273 294247
www.brighton-hove.gov.uk/content/children-and-education/youth-service/youth-employability-service
If you are 16-18 years old and not in employment, education or training, you can access free information and advice for this service.

B&H Volunteers BHV

www.bhvolunteers.org.uk
Tel: 01273 234779
We support and encourage 16-25 year old to volunteer in their local community with other charity and community groups.

NHS Choices - Beat Exam Stress

www.nhs.uk/Livewell/childhealth615/Pages/Examstress
NHS website that has some handy tips on how to reduce exam stress. Getting good sleep, good food and exercising can help a great deal.

Healthy Teens

Physical Activity

Check out the activities listing in the swimming and sports section. There is a huge variety on offer and it has so many benefits for children and young people, it can improve mental wellbeing and physical fitness as well as reduce obesity.

The NHS recommends at least 1 hour of physical activity every day for children and young people, which should be a mix of moderate activity such as fast walking and vigorous activity like running.
www.nhs.uk/Livewell/fitness/Pages/physical-activity-guidelines-for-young-people

Relationships and Young People

Teenagers are growing, maturing and at some point will take an interest in relationships. Some teens may feel confused about whether they are gay, or what sex is all about. Some may be worried about changes in their bodies. As a parent it's not always easy to support a child growing up. But to be informed is a start.

NHS Live Well - Teen Health

www.nhs.uk/Livewell/Sexandyoungpeople
Teenagers can find out about their health, how to stay safe, common myths about pregnancy, a bodies question and answer page, acne, bereavement, advice on how to avoid peer pressure, 'it's ok to say no' and other support.

Brook Advice Clinic

www.brook.org.uk
Confidential advice on sexual health for the under 25s.

Bullying

www.eastsussex.gov.uk/educationandlearning/schools/safetyandwelfare/bullying/default.htm
The East Sussex County Council website has useful information and advice. There are things that can be done to reduce or avoid bullying or being bullied. A child who avoids school, or becomes withdrawn, more anxious or aggressive may be experiencing bullying. You can also contact your child's school directly if you are at all concerned. See the section on computers for advice on online bullying.

General Support & Advice

Samaritans

24 hour telephone line: 08457 909090
www.samaritans.org

Concern about Abuse

If you are concerned or suspect abuse, that a child may be suffering physical, sexual or emotional abuse or neglect, or if as a parent or carer you feel that you may harm your child, then contact the East Sussex Child Protection Team on 01323 747373 between 8am to 6pm Monday to Friday. Outside of these hours, the Emergency Duty Team is on 01273 335905 or the police 999.

The Team's website has more information on the signs of harm and what to do if you are at all concerned.
www.eastsussex.gov.uk/childrenandfamilies/childprotection/default.htm

You can also contact the NSPCC and young people can contact Childline (details in previous page).

Stop it Now!

Tel: 0808 10000 900

Help@stopitnow.org.uk
www.stopitnow.org.uk
A campaign to prevent child sexual abuse. It has a lot of advice and information.

Domestic Violence

Note: If you are being abused and are using a computer or phone to which your abuser has access, it is strongly recommended that you take measures to cover your activity, for example use a library or internet cafe.

National Domestic Violence Helpline

Tel: (Freephone 24hr) 0808 2000 247

RISE

PO Box 889, Brighton BN2 1GH
www.riseuk.org.uk
Tel: 01273 622 822
Please leave your name and a safe contact number for RISE to call you back.
If you need an interpreter this can be arranged for you.
If you are in danger now call 999.
This is a domestic abuse charity working in Brighton & Hove and West Sussex. It can help with refuge accommodation, counselling, housing and more.

Mankind

Tel: 01823 334 244
www.mankind.org.uk
Support for male victims of domestic abuse and domestic violence

Refuge

www.refuge.org.uk
Help for women and children facing domestic violence.

Technology and Kids

Have you ever wondered how much time to let your kids play computer games, watch TV, or whether to get an Ipad? Technology can be incredibly useful.

Kids naturally want to keep up with other kids. So what limits, if any, should you choose? There is also the cost consideration, you can't get your kid the latest phone if you have not got the money.

However there are other concerns, such as bullying online, exposure to inappropriate material, children's lack of exercise from sitting around, and spending excessive hours playing the Xbox.

Generally, the information that I've read recommends that you talk to your child about online dangers, and tell them what to do if they are worried. Explain that anything they put online could be seen by anyone, and it is important not to pass on detailed information such as their name, age or address. Use filtering software to block inappropriate sites and get to know and understand what websites they visit.

Microsoft recommends that up to at leasts the age of 10 years you should sit with your children while they use computers. As they go into the teens, to continue to supervise their activities, educate them about safe use and set clear rules. Keep the computers where you can see them rather than their bedrooms.

Here are some sources of information to help you protect your child and make up your own mind about what limits to set.

Childline - Advice for Children - Online Bullying

Tel: 0800 1111
www.childline.org.uk/Explore/Bullying/Pages/online-bullying

NSPCC Keeping Your Child Safe Online

www.nspcc.org.uk/help-and-advice/for-parents/keeping-your-child-safe

Microsoft Age-based Guidelines for Kids' Internet Use

www.microsoft.com/en-gb/security/family-safety/childsafety-age

Think U Know

www.thinkuknow.co.uk
Website for kids about online safety.

Online Fun and Games for Kids

Cbeebies

www.bbc.co.uk
Toddler TV, education, fun & games from the BBC.

CBBC

www.bbc.co.uk/cbbc
Children's TV, education and fun.

Guinness World Records

www.guinnessworldrecords.com

Haring Kids

www.haringkids.com
Interactive site with online colouring and animation.

How Stuff Works

www.howstuffworks.com
Informative, interesting website that will widen your child's world.

Switch Zoo

www.switchzoo.com
Make new animals by switching bodies and heads.

Travelling with Children

It can help to think ahead when it comes to travelling with children. A baby needs a lot of equipment, a buggy and if bottle fed, formula and bottles. Toddler routines may get upset and teenagers may get bored. But do not be disheartened! It is possible to have a lot of fun with a bit of patience and practical help.

Travel Light - This may seem impossible, but it can really help not to have to

lug a lot of bags. Check if hotels have travel cots ahead.

Toys/Games - If possible, try to bring only those that will really get a lot of use. Although pack an extra surprise book or toy in case. Kids can have their own bag.

Pack for Delays - Include extra nappies, snacks, change of clothes, colouring book.

Flying - Be prepared with liquids in a separate clear bag. Baby food/formula is allowed. Take a good, collapsible buggy.

Be Realistic - Allow for the fact that you have kids and don't expect too much out of yourself or them. Sometimes it's the simplest things about travelling that are the best, so enjoy!

Equality and Diversity

Black and ethnic minority young people's project
www.bmeypp.org.uk
Tel: 01273 609298
Young peoples project providing activites and support for Black and Minority ethnic young people aged 11 to 25.

MOSAIC - Black and Mixed Parentage Family Group
Tel: 01273 234017
info@mosaicbrighton.org.uk
www.mosaicbrighton.org.uk
A community organisation of black, minority ethnic and mixed parentage families and individuals. Mosiaic Under 5's Group meets weekly in Brighton for accompanied children 0 - 5 yrs. Facilities include a soft room and outside play space.

Adoption and Fostering
Tel: 01273 295444
www.fosteringinbrightonandhove.org.uk
Brighton and Hove City Council have a Foster Carer's Handbook. They continually need to find new foster carers from all the ethnic and cultural communities.

Local Groups

AMAZE
Tel 01273 772289
www.amazebrighton.org.uk
Information, advice & support to parents/carers of children with special needs or disabilities.

Brighton Oasis project
Tel: 01273 696970
www.oasisproject.org.uk
Project for women drug users and their children, including groups, key working, recreational activities, open access, drop ins, sex work outreach, crèche, and service for 8-16 year olds affected by familial drug use.

Dads
www.brighton-hove.gov.uk/dads
Find out what's going on for dads in the city, including Baby Boogie at Jubilee Library, groups at community and children's centres and parenting courses.

Kaleidoscope
Tel: 01273 549813
www.kaleidoscopekids.org.uk
Kaleidoscope supports parents of and children with physical disabilities.

The Family Worshop
www.thefamilyworkshop.org.uk
Tel: 01273 470805
Family therapy. Counselling and other therapeutic services to children, young people, adults and families negotiating difficulties in life.

The Link Up project
www.linkupbrighton.org
Tel: 01273 678852
Supports children and young people and their families who attend mainstream education and are on the special needs registration.

MOSAIC
www.mosaicqualities.org.uk
Tel: 01273 234017
MOSAIC Black, Asian & Mixed parentage Family Group aims to provide support to BAMP people in the B&H area.

Rainbow Families
info@rainbowfamilies.org.uk
www.rainbowfamilies.org.uk
An informal social group supporting LGBT (Lesbian, Gay, Bisexual, Transgender) parents and their children
in Brighton & Hove.

Young Parents

B&H Parents and Children's Group
Tel: 01273 540717
This has summer outings, kid's art club, homework club and Christmas events.

ESSENTIAL INFORMATION

Healthcare

You should call the NHS 111 service if you need medical help fast, but it's not a 999 emergency.

You will be assessed, given advice and directed straight away to the local service that can help you best. Calls to NHS 111 are free from landlines and mobile phones.

NHS Choices

This is a very useful place to start if you want to locate a doctor, dentist, health service or are just want information.
www.nhs.uk

NHS Walk-in Centre

Brighton Station Health Centre

Aspect House
84-87 Queens Road
Brighton BN1 3XE
Tel: 01273 769 523

Photo by Nigel Lu

www.brightonstationhealthcentre.nhs.uk/our-walk-service
This walk-in service offers treatment, information and advice for a range of minor illnesses and injuries. It is open every day 8am-8pm, including bank holidays.

Hospitals

Royal Sussex County Hospital

Eastern Road
Brighton BN2 5BE
Tel: 01273 696955

Royal Alexandra Children's Hospital

Eastern Road
Brighton BN2 5BE
Tel: 01273-696955

Princess Royal Hospital

Lewes Road
Haywards Heath
West Sussex RH16 4EX
Tel: 01444 441881

Eastbourne District General Hospital

Kings Drive, Eastbourne
East Sussex, BN21 2UD
Tel: 01323 417400
www.esh.nhs.uk/hospitals/eastbournedgh/

Worthing Hospital

Lyndhurst Road, Worthing
West Sussex BN11 2DH
Tel: 01903 205111

Lewes Victoria Hospital

Nevill Road, Lewes,
East Sussex, BN7 1PE
www.esht.nhs.uk/lewes
Tel: 01273 474153

Sussex Police

Call 999 if:
- A crime is being committed now.
- The offender is still there or nearby.
- People are injured or in danger.

General Phone Enquiries
(less urgent crime enquiry)
Tel: 101 (24 hours, 7 day a week)(calls
cost a flat rate of 15p per call in UK)

Sussex Police Headquarters Church
Lane, Lewes,
East Sussex BN7 2DZ
contact.centre@sussex.pnn.police.uk
www.sussex.police.uk/help-centre/contact-us

Fire and Rescue Service

For general enquiries and fire preven-
tion advice in Sussex.
Tel 0845 130 8855 (in an Emergency
999)
www.esfrs.org

Gas Emergency

Gas emergency: 0800 111 999

Housing

There are several accommodation
agencies and estate agents. In
recent years new homes have been
built, particularly flats.

Brighton & Hove City Council

Bartholomew Square
Brighton BN1 1PF
Tel: 01273 294400
www.brighton-
hove.gov.uk/content/housing/general-
housing
Housing Advice service which offers
free, confidential advice.

Brighton Housing Trust

Community Base
113 Queens Road,
Brighton, BN1 3XG
Tel: 01273 234737
www.bht.org.uk/services/brighton-advice-
centre/
Can offer advice on with specific
housing problems.

Money

Money gets tighter with children.
There are some good advice
organisations if you are getting into
debt, such as your local Citizens
Advice Centre (on the next page).
The website Money Saving Expert
is also useful for budgeting and
saving money:
www.moneysavingexpert.com

MACS (Money Advice and Community Support)

Advice Line on 01273 664040
www.macss.org.uk
Confidential and impartial
money advice, on managing debt,
budgeting and other
finance related issues.

Tourist Information

Visitor Information Contact Centre

Tel: 01273 290337
visitor.info@visitbrighton.com
www.visitbrighton.com
Opening Hours: All year: Mon-Sat
-10.00-16.00, plus summer Sundays &
Bank Holidays.
There is a network of 14 staffed Visitor Information Points across the city
centre, offering help and advice. They
also have a good selection of free liter-
ature and maps:

- Brighton Centre Box Office, King's
  Road
- Brighton Station Travel Centre,
  Queens Road
- Brighton Toy & Model Museum,
  Trafalgar Street
- Jubilee Library, Jubilee Street
- Thistle Brighton Hotel, King's Road
- Grosvenor G Casino, King's Road
- Churchill Square, Western Road
- St Paul's Church, West Street
- Best Western Brighton Hotel, King's
  Road
- The Amsterdam Hotel, Marine Pa-
  rade
- The Old Market, Upper Market
  Street, Hove
- Oh So Swedish, Lower Promenade,
  Madeira Drive
- Royal Pavilion Shop, Pavilion Build-
  ings
- Brighton Pier, Madeira Drive

Travel

Brighton is under an hour from
London and half an hour from
Gatwick Airport.

There are excellent websites that
can give you public transport
and/or car journey details. Just
type in the start address and finish
address or postcode and time and
it will give you a detailed break-
down of trains/buses and walking
times.
www.travelinesoutheast.org.uk

Google maps is also very useful, in
giving you time and directions by car,
by foot or by cycling.
maps.google.com

Gatwick Airport

West Sussex RH6 0NP
Live flight information: 0844 892 0322
www.gatwickairport.com
The airport is 30 minutes by train, and
has a south and a north terminal. It is
well connected with international and
national flights. It is the UK's second
largest airport.

Shoreham Airport

www.flybrighton.com
Small airport. Chartered and
scheduled flights using light aircraft, 9

miles west of Brighton near the town of Shoreham-by-Sea.

Brighton & Hove Bus Company

26 North Street, Brighton
Tel: 01273 886200
www.buses.co.uk

2014 prices - Child Fares

BusID cards are issued free to young people aged 5-18 and who are permanent residents in the Brighton & Hove area. Kids travel for 40p one way with an adult. 4 years and under travel free.

Adult Fares

Short hop fares are available throughout the city for £1.80. There is a central zone flat fare of £2.

Days Out on the Bus

Go to Devil's Dyke on the 77; Stanmer Park on the 78;
Ditchling Beacon on the 79.
The Coaster 12 Brighton to Eastbourne is a nice coastal route.

Discovery fares - one day tickets (available from the bus driver):
Discovery sunset
Adult Discovery - £8.50
Child Discovery - £7 (aged 5 - 15)
Family Discovery - £16 (for 5 people with a minimum of 1 adult and a maximum of 2 adults).
Beachy Head and Sussex Downlander. From £14, travel to as many places in the South Downs in one day as you wish using train services provided by Southern and bus services from main companies.

National Express

Tel: 08717 818178

www.nationalexpress.com/wherewego/townsandcities/coach-travel-to-brighton

Bus - Park & Ride

There is a site at Withdean Sports Complex, postcode BN1 5JD. Service 27 starts from Tongdean Lane adjacent to the Sports Complex, and runs every 15 mins weekdays, 30 mins at weekends.

Please note: There is no charge for parking and the Park & Ride site is not available for overnight parking.

By Foot

Brighton and Hove are relatively compact. The Council encourages walking including walking to school. Try www.walkit.com/brighton to see your route and even calories burned.

By Bike

There number of people cycling in Brighton and Hove has grown over the last few years. There are cycle lanes around the city, including the seafront, Grand Avenue, The Drive and Hove to Hangleton. There is a map on Brighton and Hove Council's website.

ww3.brighton-hove.gov.uk/index.cfm?request=c1241435&node=20546

Cycle Training

Brighton and Hove City Council runs Bikeability training courses for children in school years five to nine. There are also free courses for children during the school holidays. To book a place call 01273 293847

www.brighton-hove.gov.uk/content/parking-and-travel/travel-transport-and-road-safety/cycle-training

Car

Gatwick Airport, coastal towns such as Eastbourne, inland villages are all accessible easily by car. London is about 50 miles, and can take 90 minutes depending on the traffic on the A23/M23.

Parking: There are several car parks, the main city Council run sites are in the Lanes, Regency Square, Trafalgar Street, Kings Road (pay and display), and in Hove: Haddington St, King Alfred, Norton Road and Kingsway (pay and display). There are car parks in London Road, Kemptown and Rottingdean. The Council have a map of street parking charges as a pdf, downloadable from their website.
www.brighton-hove.gov.uk/content/parking-and-travel/parking/pay-and-display

Train

Brighton Train Station is right in the city centre, 15 minutes walk from the beach in the North Laines area. It is on Queen's Road, housed in a grade II listed building. It has direct links to London, Gatwick Airport and the south coast. Hove Station is only a couple of minutes by train.
National Rail Enquiry Service
Tel: 08457 484950
www.nationalrail.co.uk

Traveline - 0871 200 2233
www.traveline.org.uk

Taxis

The two largest cab firms in **Brighton:**

Streamline Tel: 01273 747474 or 202020

Radio Tel: 01223 204060

However there are many taxi ranks, at the train station and in the city centre. Likewise, there are many other taxis firms in the surrounding area, but for convenience there are some listed here.

Work

The internet, local newspaper and employment agencies are all good places to start if you are looking for work.

The Argus - News Jobs
www.theargus.co.uk/jobs/

Jobs Brighton website
http://jobs.brighton.co.uk/

Brighton What's On
http://whatson.brighton.co.uk/

Unemployed/Parental Benefits

Brighton & Hove Citizens Advice Bureau

1 Tisbury Rd
Hove, United Kingdom
Tel: 845 120 3710
www.brightonhovecab.org.uk

Advice Brighton

www.advicebrighton-hove.org.uk
If you are looking for local advice services
.

Lewes Citizens Advice

3 North Ct Lewes
+44 1273 473082

Burgess Hill

www.citizensadvice.org.uk/huntscab-2
38 Church Rd
Burgess Hill, United Kingdom
+44 844 477 1171
For one to one advice and information.

Jobcentre Plus

Freephone 0800 0556688
www.direct.gov.uk.

Statutory Maternity Pay

You can get Statutory Maternity Pay if you have been working for the same employer for at least 26 weeks, by the time you are 15 weeks away from the date your baby is due. This means that you must have worked for the same employer throughout your pregnancy. It is paid by your employer if you are away from work to have a baby. It can be paid for up to 39 weeks

Maternity Allowance

You must have been working for at least 26 weeks in the 66 weeks before you are due to give birth. The rules about the benefits you can claim in pregnancy and early maternity are complicated. It is worth contacting the Citizens Advice Bureau or Jobcentre Plus.

Statutory Paternity Pay

If you are a working father, or the partner of a woman having a child (including a same-sex partner), you may be able to get Statutory Paternity Pay for two weeks during your paternity leave.

Parental Leave

Men and women both have the right to take unpaid time off work as parental leave if they have worked for their employer for one year.

Child Benefit and Child Tax Credit

Child Benefit is a tax-free benefit paid to most people with children.

Child Tax Credit is a payment for people with children, whether they are in or out of work. It is paid by HM Revenue and Customs. You can get Child Tax Credit if your income is low enough and you are responsible for at least one child.

St Luke's Advice Service

Exeter Street, Brighton
www.stlukesadviceservice.org.uk
Tel: 01273 549203
Advice on legal, housing and family matters. Open Mon, Tues, Weds and Thurs 9.30am – 3.30pm and Fri 9.30am – 1pm. Appointment only.

Brighton Unemployed Centre Families Project

Tilbury Place, Brighton
www.bucfp.org
Tel: 01273 676171
Advice on benefit issues, form filling, tribunals, problems with debts and what rights people are entitled to.
Drop-in Mon – Thurs
10.30am – 1pm & Mon – Fri 2 – 4pm.

Brighton Housing Trust

Tel 01273 234737
advice@bht.org.uk
www.bht.org.uk
Provides practical and preventative services, advice, information and guidance on housing issues.
.

Index

REFERENCES & ATTRIBUTIONS

Articles & Information

Information sourced from articles from Wikipedia - http://en.wikipedia.org

Text is available under the Creative Commons Attribution-ShareAlike License; additional terms may apply. Wikipedia® is a registered trademark of the Wikimedia Foundation, Inc., a non-profit organization. http://en.wikipedia.org/wiki/Wikipedia:Text_of_Creative _Commons_Attribution ShareAlike_3.0_Unported_License

http://en.wikipedia.org/**wiki/Brighton**
This page was last modified on 30 November 2014 at 19:26.
http://en.wikipedia.org/**wiki/Lewes**
This page was last modified on 26 November 2014 at 22:06.
http://en.wikipedia.org/**wiki/South_Downs**
This page was last modified on 13 November 2014 at 19:06.
http://en.wikipedia.org/**wiki/List_of_people_from_Brighton_ and_Hove**
This page was last modified on 26 November 2014 at 16:20.
http://en.wikipedia.org/**wiki/List_of_peoplefrom_Lewes,_Eas t_Sussex**
This page was last modified on 20 October 2014 at 17:26.
http://en.wikipedia.org/**wiki/Hove**
This page was last modified on 4 October 2014 at 01:22.
http://en.wikipedia.org/**wiki/List_of_films_set_in_Brighton**
This page was last modified on 16 September 2014 at 16:35.
http://en.wikipedia.org/**wiki/History_of_Brighton**
This page was last modified on 4 September 2014 at 03:27.

Maps

Contains Ordnance Survey data © Crown Copyright and database
right 2014 used under the OS OpenData license.

Also contains © OpenStreetMap data available under the Open Database License.
www.ordnancesurvey.co.uk/business-and-government
www.openstreetmap.org/copyright

Photographs

All photo's cited below are not owned or created by the author. Those listed here are in the public domain, using creative commons license. See copyright notice on contents pages. The use of these photos does not imply endorsement of this publication by the author or the affirmer. CC0 1.0 Universal (CC0 1.0)

Public Domain Dedication
http://creativecommons.org/publicdomain/zero/1.0/
Unsplash Public Use Photographs -
https://unsplash.com/
Page 29 - Davide Ragusa
Page 38 - Victoria Alexander
Page 39 - Andre Koch
Page 43 - Jonas Neilson Lee
Page 44 - Oisin Conolly
Page 47- David Marcu
Page 49 - Martin Dorsch
Page 51 - Jason Long
Page 57 - Tirza van Dijk
Page 100 - Ben Moore
Page 106 - Nigel Lu

Photos via Wikimedia Commons - http://commons.wikimedia.org/wiki/Main_Page
Creative Commons Public Domain Licenses
http://creativecommons.org/licenses/by-sa/2.0

Page 15 - Panorama of Hove Park from South East corner. By Hurk87 (Own work) [Public domain], via Wikimedia Commons;
http://commons.wikimedia.org/wiki/File%3AHove-park.jpg; 09/04/2010

Page 16 - Queen's Park in Brighton By A bit iffy (Own work) [Public domain], via Wikimedia Commons;
http://commons.wikimedia.org/wiki/File%3AQueens_Park_Brighton_d.jpg; http://en.wikipedia.org/wiki/User:A_bit_iffy?uselang=en-gb#Licensing_etc.;
28/04/2007

Page 20 - Preston Manor, Preston Drove By The Voice of Hassocks (Own work) [Public domain], via Wikimedia Commons;
http://commons.wikimedia.org/wiki/User:Hassocks5489?uselang=en-gb;
http://commons.wikimedia.org/wiki/File%3APreston_Manor%2C_Preston_Village%2C_Brighton_(IoE_Code_481074).jpg; 24/08/2010

Page 25 - The west front of the Royal Pavilion in Brighton by Augustus Pugim senior, 1824;
http://commons.wikimedia.org/w/index.php?title=User:Merchbow&action=edit&redlink=1&uselang=en-gb; 22/02/2006

Page 25 - Entrance Lodge to Sheffield Park in Fletching, East Sussex, England. By Charlesdrakew (Own work) [Public domain], via Wikimedia
Commons; http://commons.wikimedia.org/wiki/User:Charlesdrakew?uselang=en-gb; http://upload.wikimedia.org/wikipedia/commons/0/0f/Fletching_6.JPG;
18/07/2008

Page 26 - The Banqueting Room at the Royal Pavilion in Brighton from John Nash's "Views of the Royal Pavilion" (1826);
http://commons.wikimedia.org/w/index.php?title=User:Merchbow&action=edit&redlink=1&uselang=en-gb; 22/02/2006

Page 28 - The Chain Pier at Brighton, Royal Pavilion by J. M. W. Turner [Public domain], via Wikimedia Commons;
http://commons.wikimedia.org/wiki/File:JMW_Turner,_The_Chain_Pier_at_Brighton,_Royal_Pavilion.jpg?uselang=en-gb;
http://commons.wikimedia.org/wiki/User:Wmpearl?uselang=en-gb

Page 33 - Bodiam Castle By Tony Grist (Photographer's own files) [Public domain], via Wikimedia Commons;
http://upload.wikimedia.org/wikipedia/commons/0/04/Bodiam_Castle_1.jpg; http://commons.wikimedia.org/wiki/User:Poliphilo?uselang=en-gb; 02/03/2010

**Page 34 - Jack and Jill Mills, Clayton, showing the roundhouse of Duncton Mill. Jack stopped working in 1908 so picture is before that date.
Card postally used 4-7-1924** See page for author [Public domain], via Wikimedia Commons;
http://commons.wikimedia.org/wiki/User:Mjroots?uselang=en-gb; http://upload.wikimedia.org/wikipedia/commons/8/8c/Clayton_Duncton.jpg

Page 36 - Poster of Daddy Long Legs, unusual seagoing railway that existed in Brighton, UK, brtween 1896 and 1901 See page for author
[Public domain], via Wikimedia Common; http://commons.wikimedia.org/wiki/User:Kneiphof?uselang=en-gb;
http://upload.wikimedia.org/wikipedia/commons/d/d7/Daddylonglegs_poster.jpg;

Page 37 - The museum building at Fishbourne Roman Palace, West Sussex, England By Charlesdrakew (Own work) [Public domain], via Wikimedia Commons; http://commons.wikimedia.org/wiki/User:Charlesdrakew?uselang=en-gb;
http://upload.wikimedia.org/wikipedia/commons/7/75/Fishbourne_palace_north_wing.JPG; 09/09/2008

Page 46 - Plate XIV. from W. S. Coleman's British Butterflies (1860) By Keith Edkins (W. S. Coleman's British Butterflies) [Public domain], via
Wikimedia Commons; http://upload.wikimedia.org/wikipedia/commons/6/6e/Colemans_British_Butterflies_Plate_XIV.png; 11/10/2010

Page 46 - Plate III. from W. S. Coleman's British Butterflies (1860) By Keith Edkins (W. S. Coleman's British Butterflies) [Public domain], via
Wikimedia Commons; http://commons.wikimedia.org/wiki/File%3AColemans_British_Butterflies_Plate_III.png;
http://commons.wikimedia.org/wiki/User:Keith_Edkins?uselang=en-gb; 11/10/2010

Page 53 - Udsigt over Lewes fra Lewes Castle By Missjensen at da.wikipedia (Own work) [Public domain], via Wikimedia Commons
http://commons.wikimedia.org/wiki/File%3ALewes-udsigt.jpg; http://commons.wikimedia.org/wiki/User:MGA73bot; 1 March 2008 (original upload date)

Page 53 - Anne of Cleves House, Lewes, East Sussex By Charlesdrakew (Own work) [Public domain], via Wikimedia Commons;
http://commons.wikimedia.org/wiki/File%3ALewes_Anne_of_Cleves_House_2.JPG; http://commons.wikimedia.org/wiki/User:Charlesdrakew?uselang=en-gb;
19 September 2009

Page 55 - The Pells Swimming Pool By Charlesdrakew (Own work) [Public domain], via Wikimedia Commons;
http://commons.wikimedia.org/wiki/File%3ALewes_The_Pells_Swimming_Pool_2.JPG; http://commons.wikimedia.org/wiki/User:Charlesdrakew; 19/09/2009

Page 54 - Plan of the Battle of Lewes from *The Art of War in the Middle Ages* **by Sir Charles Oman, 1898. Uploaded by Lampman** (talk | con-
tribs); This image (or other media file) is in the public domain because its copyright has expired.;
http://commons.wikimedia.org/wiki/File:Lewes.jpg; 19/05/2007

Page 56 - Lewes railway station; Uploaded by Lamberhurst; Postally used 1920s; Author Unknown;
http://commons.wikimedia.org/wiki/File:Lewes_railway_station.jpg

Page 58 - Recreation of Battle of Hastings, Hastings By Antonio Borrillo (Own work) [Public domain], via Wikimedia Commons;
http://commons.wikimedia.org/wiki/File%3ABattle_of_hastings.JPG; http://commons.wikimedia.org/wiki/User:Antobbo_pix?uselang=en-gb; 10/10/2009

Page 94 - Sleeping cat on the floor from Khamaileon Public Domain via Wikimedia Commons;;
http://commons.wikimedia.org/wiki/File:Sleeping_cat.jpg?uselang=en-gb;